W9-BZX-537

They WALKED *in the* SPIRIT

They WALKED in the SPIRIT

PERSONAL FAITH AND SOCIAL ACTION IN AMERICA

DOUGLAS M. STRONG

Westminster John Knox Press
Louisville, Kentucky

© 1997 Douglas M. Strong

All rights reserved.
No part of this book may be reproduced or
transmitted in any form or by any means, electronic or mechanical,
including photocopying, recording, or by any information storage or
retrieval system, without permission in writing from the publisher.
For information, address Westminster John Knox Press,
100 Witherspoon Street, Louisville, Kentucky 40202-1396.

Book design by Jennifer K. Cox
Cover design by Alec Bartsch

First edition
Published by Westminster John Knox Press
Louisville, Kentucky

This book is printed on acid-free paper that meets the
American National Standards Institute Z39.48 standard. ∞

PRINTED IN THE UNITED STATES OF AMERICA
97 98 99 00 01 02 03 04 05 06 — 10 9 8 7 6 5 4 3 2 1

Library of Congress Cataloging-in-Publication Data

Strong, Douglas M., 1956–
    They walked in the Spirit : personal faith and social action in
America / Douglas M. Strong. — 1st ed.
        p.   cm.
    Includes bibliographical references.
    ISBN 0-664-25706-2 (alk. paper)
    1. Protestant churches—United States—Biography.
2. Evangelicalism—United States—History. 3. Church and social
problems—United States—History—19th century. 4. Church and
social problems—United States—History—20th century. 5. Political
activists—United States—Biography. 6. Human rights workers—
United States—Biography. I. Title.
BR569.S89   1997
280'.4'092273   dc21
    [B]   97-23722

for Cindy

Contents

Preface

W hile speaking at a regional gathering of lay people, pastors, and denominational leaders, I referred to historian Martin Marty's interpretative description of twentieth-century American Protestantism as a "two-party system."[1] Marty suggests that the Protestant church in the United States has been divided since the late nineteenth century into two "parties"—somewhat analogous to the nation's political parties. These two religious parties exist within each of the major mainline denominations. One is made up of liberals who are committed to the social gospel and concerned with the impact of religion in the public sphere. The other consists of cultural and theological conservatives who are evangelical in disposition and concerned with private faith, individual morality, and personal evangelism.

Although Marty's thesis has been accepted generally by American religious historians, most of the participants at the conference had never heard of it. During the question period that followed my lecture and in subsequent conversations, many people wanted to pursue further the idea of two parties. The topic captivated them; by their own account, they finally had a descriptive handle that they could use to interpret their experience as mainline Protestants. The concept accurately depicted their perception of the divided situation in their denominations, the contentiousness within their local churches, and even the internal tensions within their own religious life. Because I am a historian, they called upon me to provide examples of people from our Protestant heritage who had bridged the chasm between the parties.

In contrast to the excited reaction of most of those who attended the conference, a denominational officer was not pleased with my comments. He declared that the church simply did not have a split such as the one I had portrayed. Moreover, following my speech, he implied that anyone

who described the church in such terms was sowing the seeds of denominational schism. Perhaps he felt that by clearly expressing longstanding po-
larities of opinion, the problem was made worse—a legitimate fear of one
charged with the administration of a diverse denomination. But whether or
not ecclesial leaders want to admit that there is a dispute in the church between those who stress personal piety and those who stress social justice,
most thoughtful Christians know that a disagreement exists. Increasing
numbers of church people want to acknowledge the tension, and because
there is a deep hunger for a holistic spirituality—one that integrates personal faith and social action—they want to know how they can embrace
both aspects of Christian praxis.

This book endeavors to acknowledge and surmount the factional division in American Protestantism. While I recognize that a two-party mind-
set has been operating within the church for over a century, I also bring to
light a narrative history of the courageous souls who have labored in the
gospel in such a way as to overcome the effects of that mind-set. This volume features the stories of American Protestants who during the last one
hundred and fifty years exemplified a holistic spirituality. Each of them nurtured a profoundly deep relationship with Christ and simultaneously
worked for the transformation of society, thereby transcending the pub-
lic/private split in American Protestantism. The result is an anthology of
religious biographies centering on figures who have combined social witness and evangelical faith.

There are dangers in lifting up historical models. We could, for example, attempt to replicate the past or apply lessons from a different time and
culture in ways that are no longer appropriate. Nonetheless, a historical retrieval is still important—especially for pragmatically minded Americans,
who tend to value current experience and to deprecate tradition. Recount-
ing the religious heritage of the United States bears relevance for both spiritual growth and the work of social transformation. As the psalmist writes,
it is important "to number our days that we may gain a heart of wisdom"
(Ps. 90:12). The study of the past prepares us for "the living of these days."

I hope to accomplish several goals with this project of historical recovery. First, these biographies will assist church historians in appreciating nu-
ances and making room for exceptions to their interpretative schema, so
that historical figures who do not conform to standard analytical categories
will be recognized for their importance and their impact on American
Christianity. Most of the persons featured in this book are not well-known
today; nonetheless, they were influential integrators of faith and social justice. I believe that the reason some of them are unknown is precisely because they demonstrated an integrated Christian life; they do not fit into
the neat historical categories of "fundamentalist" or "modernist," "liberal"
or "conservative."

Some of the religious amalgamations exhibited in the lives of the people portrayed in this book may appear to us to be strange bedfellows. However, they should remind us that we dare not succumb to religious stereotyping when characterizing persons in the past (or those in the present, for that matter). We must be careful, for instance, not to identify "piety" with "conservative," or "social gospel" with "liberal." Despite the essential validity of Marty's two-party characterization of American Protestantism, some Christians defied the prevalent polarization of piety and justice. While many advocates of the social gospel were theologically liberal, for example, others were not. And while pietistic Christians have tended to be theologically conservative, they may or may not have been conservative on political or social issues. In fact, in the nineteenth century, both those who were most progressive on issues of race and gender and those who were most conservative on the same issues regarded their evangelical conversion experiences to be the crucial events of their religious lives.

My second goal concerns my hopes for the church. I hope that these biographical portraits will encourage social activists to remember the zeal of their affective relationship with Christ, so that they will not have a rootless activism. I also hope that the biographies will encourage pietistically minded Christians to become more engaged in the world, so that they will not have a hollow piety. The essence of spirituality must be understood as the whole experience of God, discerned personally and corporately, for without both inner experience and outward action we are not fully Christian. For those readers who are already seeking to balance prayer and action, the lives here represented may be able to provide new theological insights and a fresh frame of reference—from the vantage point of the past.

There is also an ecumenical relevance for the retelling of these stories. More and more, religious leaders involved in interconfessional dialogue realize the importance of various faith traditions recognizing each other's "saints," those people who should be lifted up as faithful examples for the edification of the whole church. This book probes to the heart of a particular faith tradition—American Protestantism—and specifically directs attention to some of the unsung heroes within that tradition, but it does so for the benefit of all Christians.

I have chosen to approach this subject through the perspective of biography rather than through a more typical linear historical account because, in an age in which cynicism and distrust abound toward institutions of all kinds, authenticity remains regarding an individual's life. The stories of actual people who endeavored to lead faithful lives in the past assist us in valuing our own potential for influencing the church and the world—despite their (and our) limitations due to personality and culture.

In order to be representative of U.S. Protestant culture, this anthology must be broadly inclusive. I chose figures specifically for their diversity.

Included are women and men; Northerners and Southerners; laity and clergy; persons from rich, poor, and middle-class backgrounds; persons from various ethnic roots—European American, African American, and Hispanic American; and persons from several different denominational families—Baptist, Congregational, Disciples of Christ, Episcopalian, Methodist, and Presbyterian. Among them, the individuals represent a variety of social movements: abolitionism, the temperance movement, women's rights, the social gospel, the Progressive movement, the industrial democracy movement, the ecumenical movement, the settlement house movement, Christian socialism, the missionary movement, communitarianism, and the civil rights movement. They also represent extremely varied religious traditions (each of which will be discussed in the text): perfectionistic revivalism, the Holiness movement, Pentecostalism, African American spirituality, postmillennialism, premillennialism, realized eschatology, liberalism, Anglo-Catholic mysticism, Southern Baptist piety, neo-evangelicalism, and liberation theology. In addition, the influence of their lifework ranged over an extended time period: the active ministry of the people highlighted in this book encompassed one hundred and fifty years—from William Goodell's politicization of the antislavery movement in 1837 to the career of theologian Orlando Costas, who died in 1987.

Some may question why I have focused only on North Americans. Indeed, during the second half of the twentieth century, some of the most notable examples of holistic praxis have come to us from the developing world—Latin Americans such as Gustavo Gutiérrez and Oscar Romero, Africans such as Mercy Oduyoye and Desmond Tutu, and Asians such as Toyohiko Kagawa and Daniel Thambyrajah Niles. It is imperative that we listen to the voices of these modern-day prophets, for we need to hear the corrective challenge and critique of our culture from persons outside of it, many of whom are able to assess our religious life more accurately than we can.

Nonetheless, we also need models of persons who have lived a holistic gospel *within* our culture. This is the context in which we live and work, the society that we are called upon to encounter with the gospel of Christ. Must we reject American Christian history wholesale as hopelessly flawed? Is there a "usable past" from the religious heritage of the United States? I contend that we need historical examples of vital piety and social concern specifically from our North American milieu. Only people from the United States have had to deal with the unique experience of a multicultural, consumerist society located in a nation in which the religious ghosts of the past fight for dominance with the secular pretensions of the present. The persons in this volume lived and worked in this particular environment, struggling with a culture that has accentuated the dichotomy between social activism and the spiritual life. Interpreting their Christian lives serves the present-day spiritual formation of those of us in the United States who are similarly struggling Christians. This study, then, is a critical appropriation of the North American Protestant tradition for today—specifically, the spiritual resources provided within U.S. Protestantism for the task of social transformation.

Others may wonder what could possibly unify these various Protestants, especially since they came from such divergent spiritual traditions and varied ethnocultural experiences. How can the spiritual practice and social witness of women or people of color, for instance, be assembled in the same collection with the occurrences of persons who came from culturally hegemonic groups? Should not the distinctive spiritualities of marginalized persons be treated separately, in order that their voices will not be subsumed into the religious monotones of the dominant culture?

Perhaps not. In the first place, in a society where the interrelationship of people from many cultures is a matter of fact, dialogue between groups is essential. Among those who profess Jesus Christ, such dialogue is a gospel imperative. It is important that we learn together about our different religious perspectives and thereby increase our respective understandings of one another.

Secondly, there is a good historical reason for treating the various cultural groups of American Protestants in the same book. Throughout the nineteenth and twentieth centuries, a particular type of spirituality—evangelical experience—has provided a link between the various cultural expressions of U.S. Protestants. Evangelical experience is a Biblically grounded, affective appropriation of personal faith in Christ, usually connected with a crisis spiritual event in an individual's life. This particular type of spirituality has permeated nearly every cultural group within American Protestantism, and the history of Protestantism in the United States has been preeminently molded by the so-called "evangelical consensus" of the early nineteenth century. Since evangelicalism has been the prevailing theological manifestation of U.S. Protestantism for most of the last two centuries, it is important to comprehend its specific strengths and weaknesses with singular attention. It will not be surprising to discover that each figure in this anthology hailed from an evangelical background and, at least indirectly, was theologically shaped by evangelical Biblical formation and the experience of a "new birth" conversion.

If their shared encounter with evangelical faith is what tied these persons together, their vastly different life circumstances are what kept them and their theological formulations clearly distinguished from one another. Interesting combinations resulted from the melding of their spiritual experiences and their particular situational backgrounds, such as the uniting of African American religious culture and holiness spirituality in the Pentecostal social vision of William Seymour, the fusion of Anglo-Catholic mysticism, evangelicalism, and the social gospel in the ministry of Vida Scudder, and the joining of Latino liberation theology with Billy Graham style neo-evangelicalism to produce the contextual missiology of Orlando Costas.

Not every Protestant figure who could have been included in this anthology is featured here. Persons such as Frances Willard and Martin Luther King Jr. immediately come to mind, each of whom has already been featured in numerous books. I have decided to highlight people who also contributed to Protestant thought but have not been discussed as frequently. I am convinced that focusing on the devotional and social commitments of less well-known people provides case studies of "ordinary" pastors and lay people who have lived out a commitment to a balanced Christian faith during a time period (such as the present!) when such a balance was not popular or easy.

One can be a Christian and be socially involved, but it is quite another thing to have one's social involvement emanate from a substantive, clearly articulated spiritual life, in which, as William Goodell stated, the daily communion of the indwelling Christ results in "holy activity." Each of the individuals in this collection demonstrated an active social justice ministry and explicitly expressed a well-formed, theologically grounded spirituality. For these Christians, there was no distinction between the devotional life and the active life, the personal and the social, the theological and the practical, because each one centered his or her own activity on the prior creative activity of God in Christ.

The Introduction sets the historical stage for the rest of the book, providing an overview of the persons, movements, and social forces that have led to the perceived split between piety and religious social action within the American church. More precisely, I describe the history of evangelical social concern during the past two centuries as a background for the individual narratives that follow.

Chapters one through eight revolve around the life stories of specific people. A biographical vignette forms the heart of each chapter. The vignette focuses on a theme of each person's ministry, suggesting his or her particular contribution to the concept of a holistic gospel in America. (The theme is indicated by the subtitle of the chapter.) Throughout the chapters, I connect the life and career of each person to the other figures in the book and to the broader theological and social issues of the North American context.

Concluding each of the biographical chapters is a selection from the person's writings, demonstrating his or her significance to the integration of spirituality and social action. I am especially pleased about the inclusion of these primary sources, for they are neglected gems of American religious literature. For the most part, these writings have been out of print for many years. They deserve to be recovered and presented together for the spiritual enrichment of a new generation of Christians.

This book joins a number of others that have addressed the historical interrelationship of social concern and religious faith in the United States.[2] My book, however, differs from the others in two ways. First, the other books have dwelt primarily on the social action side of the polarity, in part because, given the recent history of Protestant social involvement (aligned with highly conservative causes such as the Christian Coalition), Christian scholars have often felt the need to defend the record regarding the Church's social ministry. In the process of emphasizing the credentials of these individuals in terms of their social work, however, their spiritual fervor and theological depth may have been slighted. Instead of using the social justice accomplishments of Christian reformers as a framework for understanding their religious commitments, we need to work outward from their formative faith experiences in order to understand the basic religious impetus that lay behind their social commitments. In so doing, we will give as much prominence to the affective piety of these persons as they did. Although I will review the history of religious social engagement, I will put particular stress on each figure's contribution to American spirituality in relation to her or his involvement with social issues.

Second, these biographies—spanning U.S. history from the early republic until the present—make it clear that there has been a continuous historical legacy of holistic religious practice during the past century and a half. As American Protestants, we can point proudly to a tradition (albeit small) of spiritual rootedness and social vision. Together, some of the attributes gleaned from the past may help to illuminate the pitfalls ahead and to spur us along on our own journeys toward faithful action in Christ.

NOTES

1. Martin E. Marty, *Righteous Empire: The Protestant Experience in America* (New York: Dial Press, 1970), 177–87. Marty's ideas on the "two-party system" were partially derived from the research of one of his graduate students, who later published her own account of the division in American Protestantism. See Jean Miller Schmidt, *Souls or the Social Order: The Two-Party System in American Protestantism* (Brooklyn: Carlson, 1991).

2. Primary among the books that study the connection between Protestant faith and social concern in the United States are Timothy L. Smith, *Revivalism and Social Reform* (Baltimore: Johns Hopkins University Press, 1980); Donald W. Dayton, *Discovering an Evangelical Heritage* (New York: Harper & Row, 1976); and Ronald C. White and C. Howard Hopkins, *The Social Gospel: Religion and Reform in Changing America* (Philadelphia: Temple University Press, 1976). Also important are several biographical accounts of the spiritual and social commitments of particular groups of people (for women, see Nancy

Hardesty, *Women Called to Witness: Evangelical Feminism in the 19th Century* [Nashville: Abingdon Press, 1984] and Rosemary Skinner Keller, ed., *Spirituality and Social Responsibility: The Vocational Vision of Women in the United Methodist Tradition* [Nashville: Abingdon Press, 1993]) or of people during particular eras (for the nineteenth century, see Anthony L. Dunnavent, ed., *Poverty and Ecclesiology: Nineteenth-Century Evangelicals in the Light of Liberation Theology* [Collegeville, Minn.: Liturgical Press, 1992]; for the twentieth century, see Gary Commins, *Spiritual People, Radical Lives* [San Francisco: International Scholars Publications, 1996]).

Introduction: The Mixed Legacy
of American Evangelicalism

In some respects, the concept of a public/private split in American Protestantism echoes an ancient division within Christianity. Some early movements, such as Gnosticism and Manicheanism, were notorious for the separation that they made between the temporal and the "spiritual." Orthodox spirituality, too, had a dualistic streak, especially as articulated by church fathers like Clement of Alexandria, who appropriated then-current neoplatonic distinctions between spirit and matter. Later, medieval monastics struggled with how to find an appropriate balance between the "active life" and the "contemplative life." And during the Reformation period, Lutherans arrived at a paradoxical understanding of Christian existence known as the "two kingdoms"—the material realm of sinful human institutions juxtaposed with the spiritual realm of God's divine rule.

While the tension between faith and action has been longstanding in the Christian church, and especially in the Western church, never has the polarization been so pronounced as in the United States during the nineteenth and twentieth centuries. How did the American church get to this extremely divided situation? It was not always so.

The Colonial Period

A particularly important religious influence on early America, most historians agree, came from New England Puritanism. Puritanism was an attempt to purify the Church of England by following a rigorous set of Reformation principles derived from Calvinist (also known as "Reformed") theology. In the Reformed tradition, it was expected that Christian values would be lived out in every aspect of society. John Calvin's intent was to apply the gospel to the total life of the community, for he believed that the church had been given the responsibility for shaping a Christian civilization and that earthly government must reflect the values of God's reign. In addition, each individual was responsible to God to "lead a life worthy of the calling to which you have been called" (Phil.4:1). This summons to live ethically included both a person's morals and his or her corporate life in the broader society. In short, Puritans acquired from Calvinism a theology of Christian vocation expressed in social obligation. English Puritans hoped to copy the Reformed theocracy of Calvin's Geneva in their native land. For a brief period in the mid-seventeenth century they succeeded. During these years they also attempted to establish a Calvinist "model of Christian charity" in New England that could be emulated in old England. Whether or not this Puritan experiment in the New World ever served as an exemplification of Christian charity to the Old World is open to question, but it did outlive the Puritan commonwealth in Britain by several decades.

The excesses of the Puritan theocracy in Massachusetts are infamous: those deemed to be heretics were executed; dissidents were banished; morality was enforced by law; and politics was ruled by the church. But Puritan New England society had a more positive side to it. For example, the vision of a Puritan commonwealth led to the belief that all parts of life were interrelated—family, commerce, and religious conviction. Prices were fixed so that the poor could afford basic staples. The meetinghouse became the spiritual and civil center of the community. While deviation was not allowed, community bonds were strong, and there was a connectedness between every facet of one's existence.

Puritans also emphasized the necessity of an experiential conversion to Christ. One of the "visible signs" of that conversion was the outworking of faith in good deeds to the poor. Puritans considered economic success to be a mark of hard work and frugality, but they also considered too much wealth to be a sinful sign of ostentatious pride and insensitivity to the needy. The Puritans had an organic worldview, for they had not yet encountered the nineteenth-century American segmentation between private devotion and public action.

Even after Puritan control ended in New England, the Calvinist sense of social obligation remained among eighteenth-century American Christians. That is because religious expression in the British North American colonies continued to be dominated by the spirituality of Reformed Calvinism. This theological predominance was most obvious in New England, where various strands of Calvinism persisted among the Congregationalists and the Baptists. In the South, the religious life of the established Church of England was heavily tinged with Calvinism. Even though the religious authority of the Church of England had waned by the time of the American Revolution, Reformed theology still prevailed in the southern colonies, due to the evangelistic impact of the Great Awakening (1730s–40s). As a result of the Awakening, Presbyterians and Baptists made significant inroads into Southern religious life, and they extended Calvinist influence in the region. The religious demographics of the middle colonies presented an extremely mixed situation, in which various kinds of ethnic Calvinists (Scottish Presbyterians, Dutch Reformed, German Reformed, and French Huguenots) intermingled with Lutherans, Quakers, and a few Catholics. In sum, although other religious traditions were present, Reformed theological understandings predominated in colonial religious life, and Calvinism became the primary influence on religious attitudes toward public affairs.

Jonathan Edwards (1703–1758), one of the leading religious voices of colonial America, was representative of those Reformed theologians who articulated a unitive sense of the responsibility of faith in the public sphere. Edwards synthesized social concern and private religious experience. True religion, he was convinced, began with a transformed heart. Then, however, this "religion of the heart" must be expressed in public engagement. Like eighteenth-century people generally, Edwards did not have an understanding of the effect that social structures can have on individual action; nonetheless, he believed that "inner spiritual experience and outward religious action were movements of the same soul, pieces of the same cloth."[1]

In the period after Edwards's death in the mid-eighteenth century, the religious landscape in America changed dramatically due to two important historical developments—the Enlightenment and the Industrial Revolution. The impact of these developments was experienced first in Britain, but, eventually, the American religious worldview was affected as well. The effect of the Enlightenment was felt in America by the time of independence in the 1770s, while the repercussions of the Industrial Revolution were generally not felt until the 1830s (and, in some sections of the country, not until much later). The combination of these two factors significantly altered the subsequent history of the newly established United States. Intellectually, theologically, and culturally, these developments help to mark a clear historical division between the period before the early American republic and the years since.

Enlightenment Influences:
Autonomy and Equality

The Enlightenment was an intellectual movement that helped to initiate a cultural reshaping of Western society and usher in what historians refer to as "modernity" or the "modern" period. A reaction to decades of religious warfare and dogmatic exclusivism following the Reformation, the Enlightenment issued a summons to build a society based on rational discourse, experimental testing of truth claims, and the inherent equality of all persons. The age-old contention that the absolutist rule of monarchs was necessary to curb the violent actions of depraved human beings was countered by the Enlightenment contention that "we, the people" could rule ourselves if given the freedom to do so, because we are basically good. In fact, human beings were equipped with limitless potential if left to reason for themselves. Scientific advances demonstrated that fixed laws governed the natural world; why, it was asked, could not the dissemination of knowledge assist people in discovering and applying the laws that governed human behavior and institutions? According to this optimistic view of human nature, if educated ("enlightened") people would slough off the bonds of "artificial," humanly constructed restraints and tyrannical despotism, then a "natural" state of interpersonal benevolence would prevail. Franklin, Jefferson, Madison, and most of the other "founding fathers" advanced these Enlightenment concepts through their formation of the political structures of the United States.

Perhaps most important for our purposes was the Enlightenment understanding of the individual self. Building on the Reformation principle of the priesthood of all believers and opposing the divine right of kings and other arbitrary authorities, Enlightenment thinkers posited the natural or inherent rights of all people. As a well-known, Enlightenment-influenced document declared: all people "are endowed by their Creator with certain inalienable rights." According to Jefferson's design for a democratic society, each individual was visualized as an independent unit. People were regarded as autonomous, self-determining egos who had the means to chart their own courses of action. This Enlightenment-inspired understanding of personal autonomy had both negative and positive results.

For example, the Enlightenment stress on the self-determining ego had the tendency to encourage an unrestrained individualism within Western culture. Enlightenment thinkers were inclined to believe that society was a concession to human vulnerability, a contract to restrict liberty that was entered into by individuals for practical reasons—in order to obtain the benefits of social cooperation and to maintain social order. Society was considered to be a necessary evil, to be carefully monitored so as not to inhibit personal freedom. Consequently, the perceived demands of the social contract were in tension with the emphasis on natural rights. A defining struggle in post-Revolutionary American culture was to find an appropriate balance between the two.

The Enlightenment concept of the self and its relationship to society also had a strong impact on Protestant spirituality in America. Most

Protestants would not have admitted any dependence on Enlightenment thought, for they saw themselves as enemies of the religious skepticism often associated with modernity. Nonetheless, Enlightenment ideas were evident in such nineteenth-century Protestant developments as the acceptance of lay empowerment, the popularity of congregational polity, the influence of theological free will, and the possibility of spiritual progress. Enlightenment concepts were perhaps most obvious in the evangelical concept of conversion.

Evangelicalism was a religious movement that arose in the eighteenth century, growing out of English Puritanism and continental Pietism. It stressed the primacy of the Bible as an immediate religious authority and the normativeness of a crisis conversion experience. Influenced by Enlightenment notions of autonomy, American evangelicalism—particularly in the nineteenth century—came to emphasize the role of human will in the conversion process. Every person needed to decide for him or herself whether to accept God's offer of salvation.

Another religious influence of the Enlightenment, originating from its positive view of human nature and the potential for progress, was the stress on the attainability of holiness. As holiness was originally articulated in its eighteenth-century Methodist form by John Wesley, a person could receive God's sanctifying grace, a second blessing beyond justification through which one came to love God and neighbor with "perfect" intent. Later, in the nineteenth century, continuing the Enlightenment stress on individual volition, holiness was redefined as willing what God willed— good willing or "benevolence." Sin was defined as just the opposite: not willing what God willed—even though "illumination" from God was available.

The potential goal of holiness was "a perfect state of society," a society full of individuals acting benevolently. Closely connected to this view of the perfectibility of society was an eschatological (end-times) doctrine that we describe as postmillennialism. Simply put, postmillennialists believed that Christ's second coming would follow the establishment of the millennium, Christ's rule on earth. The millennium would be the result of Christians successfully working in the world. Postmillennialism pinned great hopes on the potential of sanctified human beings to bring about God's kingdom. This religious optimism regarding the future meshed well with the general spirit of optimism prevalent in the early American republic.

Yet another way in which the Enlightenment influenced American culture was the intellectual base that it provided for the formation of national values such as equality and personal liberty. In particular, Americans were favorably impressed with the idea that all people had God-given natural rights regardless of their previous social status. As this concept caught hold of the popular imagination in the American colonies, it became evident that the traditional systems of hereditary government and hierarchical church structures inhibited the application of the new ideas. Many thought that a "new order for the ages" (in Latin, *novus ordo seclorum*, printed on every dollar bill) could be established in America, in which individual freedom and democratic principles would prevail.

This principle of the equality of all persons is the root of cherished American concepts such as self-determination, democratic freedom, and the sovereignty of the individual. Enlightenment thought was thus the chief source for our modern emphasis on equal rights, an emphasis that has been the inspiration for progressive movements from abolitionism to women's suffrage to labor reform to civil rights.

The Social Construction
of Industrial Capitalism

The second important influence on American religious life was the Industrial Revolution, which began in the United States in the 1830s and 1840s, nearly a century after it had evolved in Britain. The industrial growth was undergirded by laissez-faire capitalism, an economic policy advocated by Britain's Adam Smith. Smith taught that the "invisible hand" of Providence should be allowed to regulate the market without any interference of human regulations. The economy was a natural system that functioned best when left to itself.

Unlike a rural economy in which peasants live at least somewhat communally, share work responsibilities, and have face-to-face commodity transactions, industrial capitalism demands a concentrated labor supply and depends on the differentiation of labor into component parts. This specialization of tasks results in economic efficiency, but it also separates people from knowledge about one another's work (and, consequently, about the world in which they work) in ways that are not noticeable in an agrarian society. In America, in the rural or small town areas of New England and the mid-Atlantic states, people of varied economic levels lived in close proximity to one another and the economic range between the poor and the well-off was not large. But as urbanization developed throughout the nineteenth century, social classes became much more clearly defined. The classes were also separated demographically. Consumers were removed physically and economically from the persons who produced their goods.

The social construction that developed under industrial capitalism divided the day-to-day existence of middle-class people into highly differentiated "spheres": home (domestic life) vis-à-vis work (business life); principled values countered by expedient compromise; the sacred versus the secular; private morality or public politics; piety and virtue or economics and business. A specialization of roles developed in conjunction with the differentiation of labor associated with the growth of a market economy. The common nineteenth-century view was that there were particularly appropriate areas of influence for various groups of people within society. Differentiated roles were established, for example, for women in contrast to men, for black people in contrast to white people, and for clergy in contrast to laity. Moreover, religious practice and political action had definite, prescribed boundaries. The division of material and spiritual reality into segmented spheres was thus a product of a broader cultural understanding of the period.

Industrial growth led to other social changes that affected the religious life of the nation. Large-scale immigration and the development of labor-intensive manufacturing resulted in a massive movement to the cities, with the consequent urban problems of disease, emotional alienation, crime, concentrated poverty, and class distinctions—problems that we now know to be almost inevitably associated with a nation's capitalist expansion but that were unexpectedly new problems to the American church and society in the nineteenth century.

Voluntary Societies and Revivals

The new United States remained primarily an agrarian society until the second quarter of the nineteenth century and, in some regions, until long after that. Consequently, most Americans did not have to deal with the urban social problems associated with an industrializing society until the mid to late nineteenth century. Nonetheless, there were numerous social stresses in the new republic, especially during the period of great demographic expansion after the War of 1812. Naturally, some Americans attempted to address these social conflicts.

The first religious efforts in this direction were initiated by Lyman Beecher (1775–1863) and other leaders in the early nineteenth-century alliance of Congregationalists and Presbyterians. The two denominations combined their home missions' deployment in order to tackle the enormous task of Protestantizing the souls and the society of the frontier West in light of the perceived triple threat of Catholicism, Deistic skepticism, and immoral behavior. Beecher and his Presbyterian/Congregationalist friends designed an evangelical plan to win the trans-Appalachian West for Christ.

There were two components to their plan. First, they founded voluntary "benevolent" societies to direct a massive regional infusion of preachers, Bibles, Christian literature, and Sunday schools. They set up interdenominational organizations to fund evangelism, distribute Christian materials, and reform the morals of the populace. Examples include the American

Temperance Society, the American Tract Society, the American Sunday School Union, and the Female Moral Reform Society (an antiprostitution organization). Even the drive to establish public schools during this era was based on the premise that evangelical influence on education would help to "enlighten" the moral condition of the frontier. The leadership of the voluntary societies was linked together by interlocking directorates, often referred to as the "Benevolent Empire."

Second, Beecher and his colleagues promoted a highly successful evangelistic method known as revivalism. In the early American republic, revivals consisted of periodically held religious meetings, often of several days duration, at which all efforts were directed toward leading persons to an experience of evangelical conversion. Revivalism was a very popular religious strategy that ebbed and flowed nearly nonstop throughout the entire century. For most Protestants, revivals became the normative form of Christian initiation and church recruitment.

Scholarly opinion is divided regarding the motives and goals of revivalism and the voluntary societies. Some have concluded that the Presbyterian and Congregationalist leaders of the benevolent societies were intent primarily on "social control." According to this thesis, the success of revivalism and the Benevolent Empire was due to the fact that it provided a moral legitimation for the exercise of power at the expense of the underclass. Depending on which historian one reads, either Beecher and his colleagues were members of a declining elite of New England establishment clergy who wanted to maintain their waning power[2] or they were middle class men "on the make" who were allies of the emerging capitalization.[3] In the latter interpretation, Beecher's group promoted conservative moral values such as honesty, discipline, sobriety, and thrift in order to support the newly developing middle-class culture. Temperance, for example, was encouraged not because of Christian concern for others but because sober workers were more productive workers. Thus, the earliest beginnings of social Christianity in the United States intended to support the bourgeois needs of Presbyterian and Congregationalist shopkeepers, not to improve the social conditions of the working poor.

There are problems with these reductionistic "social control" theses.[4] In the first place, it is always difficult to gauge the actual intent of social reformers. It is more reasonable to believe that a combination of objectives— mixed motives—contributed to the rise of the voluntary societies. While social control was an important factor in the minds of many moral reformers, they also had other reasons for their actions: a genuine interest in establishing an equitable social order, for example, or the simple desire to share with others their experience of a vital relationship with Christ. There is another difficulty with the social control concept. While it seems to offer an accurate characterization of Beecher and his cohorts, the largest number of participants in the revivalism of the early nineteenth century were not derived from Beecher's middle- to upper-class Congregationalists and Presbyterians, but rather from the Methodists and Baptists, who were attracting African Americans, the poor, and other marginalized people.

No matter what interpretation is adopted regarding the ultimate purpose of revivalistic evangelicalism, it is clear that it became the characteristic expression of American Protestantism in the first quarter of the nineteenth century. That is, the major Protestant denominations all preached the normativeness of a conversion experience and the necessity of bringing their neighbors to this experience—usually through revivalism. The period before the Civil War was the religious era of the "evangelical consensus," when fully eighty percent of American church members belonged to a revivalistic evangelical church. Though these churches were highly competitive among themselves, they agreed on one thing: the necessity of being born again by the Holy Spirit to an affective relationship with God through Christ. Evangelicalism had thus become the dominant spirituality in the United States, a sort of unofficial religious establishment. By 1850, all of the largest Protestant denominations—in order, Methodist, Baptist, Presbyterian, and Congregational—were thoroughly and almost uniformly evangelical, as were several important but somewhat smaller denominations, such as the Disciples of Christ and various German-speaking groups. Even people from religious traditions that were not traditionally evangelical—Lutherans, Episcopalians, Quakers, the Dutch Reformed, and Mennonites—were strongly influenced in an evangelical direction during the nineteenth century.[5] Those groups that resisted the process of "evangelicalizing," such as the Unitarians, nonconversionist Protestants (Missouri Synod Lutherans), Shakers, Mormons, Jews, and atheists, were all very small groups. Only the Roman Catholics represented a large religious presence in the first half of the nineteenth century that was not evangelical Protestant and, as historian Jay Dolan has pointed out, even Catholics adapted to the revivalistic style of spirituality.[6] Despite some fluctuations in its influence, evangelicalism was and is the religious mind-set that continues to shape a major portion of American Christianity.

If the piety of American Protestants was clearly established by the middle of the nineteenth century, Protestantism's credentials in the area of social action were not. Because of the prevalence of the Enlightenment emphasis on privatistic self-determination and because of the general acceptance of the market economy concept of differentiated "spheres," Protestantism had become, according to the 1847 observation of Henry James Sr., "the citadel and shield of individualism." James was convinced that churchgoers manifested more of "the selfish principle" than the Golden Rule.[7] An environment was created in which churches were expected to pronounce on issues of personal faith and morality but have nothing to do with broad social policy, especially if it had political ramifications. In the United States, this religious/political compartmentalization was exacerbated by the legal separation of church and state enshrined in the First Amendment. While the "establishment clause" of the First Amendment has had broad popular support throughout American history, it has also had the potential to be misinterpreted as a Constitutional exclusion of religious and moral influence from civil matters.

Evangelicals Confront Slavery

One ethical issue became paramount and pushed some American Protestants toward a more systemic perspective on social problems. That issue was slavery, the besetting sin of the United States—sometimes referred to as America's "original sin." Eventually, it was to overshadow all other issues in importance.

Religious antislavery agitation in America proceeded in several different phases. Quakers have rightfully been credited for first drawing attention, in the eighteenth century, to the immorality of slavery. But by the early nineteenth century, Quakers were as complicitous as other Americans in slavery, both as slaveholders and as merchants whose livelihood depended on slave labor. In the years immediately after the Revolutionary War, it was Methodist, Baptist, and Presbyterian evangelicals who took bold stands against slavery. No slaveholder, for example, could be a member of the Methodist church. Soon, though, each of the evangelical denominations compromised their earlier antislavery positions. Within a few years, as these groups began to grow in slaveholding areas, their stringent rules against the church's connection with slavery were relaxed.

In the South, the desire to perpetuate slavery and the lifestyle it supported prompted whites to articulate a specific doctrine against church participation in public policy decisions. As John Holt Rice, the founder of Union Theological Seminary in Virginia, declared in 1827, "it never has fared well with either church or state, when the church meddled with temporal affairs." Rather, the church should "go on minding [its] own business, and endeavoring to make as many good Christians as possible among masters and servants." By the early 1830s, this doctrine of "the spirituality of the church" was well-established in the South, especially in the face of the growing abolitionist movement in the North and the notoriety surrounding Nat Turner's famous slave insurrection in 1831. Southern pastors began to claim that slavery was a positive good and tried to defend the institution with Biblical arguments.[8]

The strongest proponent of the spirituality of the church theory was Presbyterian theologian James Henley Thornwell (1812–1862), one of the most influential ministers in the South. Thornwell's rejection of religious "intermeddling" with the "natural order" of society paralleled Adam Smith's rejection of human manipulation with the natural order of the economy. The doctrine of the spirituality of the church was, therefore, a direct theological equivalent of laissez-faire economic theory. The church, Thornwell argued

> is not a moral institute of universal good, whose business it is to wage war upon every form of human ill. . . . It has no commission to construct society afresh. . . . The problems, which the anomalies of our fallen state are continually forcing on philanthropy, the Church has no right directly to solve. She must leave them to the Providence of God, and to human wisdom sanctified and guided by the spiritual influences which it is her glory to foster and to cherish.

Specifically, regarding the slavery issue, he insisted that the church

> has no right to interfere directly with the civil relations of society. Whether slavery shall be perpetuated or not, whether arrangements shall be made to change or abolish it, whether it conduces to the prosperity of States or hinders the progress of a refined civilization— these are questions not for the Church but for the State, not for Ministers but statesmen. Christian men may discuss them as citizens and patriots, but not as members of the Church of Jesus Christ.

Not surprisingly, Thornwell believed that God had established slavery as a providential form of labor.[9]

Charles G. Finney: Integrating Piety and Social Concern

Thornwell's foil was not only radical abolitionists such as William Lloyd Garrison (1805–79), who had rejected the church altogether, but also antislavery leaders within the church, such as his fellow Presbyterian, evangelist Charles G. Finney (1792–1875). Finney grew up and was converted in the so-called "burned-over district" of upstate New York, a region known for its sweeping fires of religious revivalism and innovative social reform.[10] During the late 1820s and early 1830s, the same period in which sectional tensions were heating up over the slavery issue, Finney's revival preaching began to be nationally known. In the winter of 1830–31, Finney preached his renowned Rochester, New York, revival, which catapulted him to national fame. Thousands of people responded to Finney's invitation to Christian conversion during his six-month stint in Rochester. But his reputation also grew because he employed controversial "new measures" in his revival campaigns. These measures included the practice of holding "protracted meetings" over several days, weeks, or even months; the use of an "anxious bench" in the front of the church where penitent sinners would gather for special attention from the evangelist and congregation; the habit of allowing women to pray publicly in "promiscuous" (gender-mixed) assemblies; and his insistence on preaching about social and moral issues, such as temperance and, eventually, the abolition of slavery.

Finney's primary message was the need for individuals to repent of their sins, to be converted to God, and to live a holy life. This last point was very important to Finney. Though a Presbyterian, Finney's view of holiness was quite similar to the Methodist interpretation of sanctification. (Not surprisingly, Finney got into trouble for this view. When his doctrinal disagreements with orthodox Calvinism were combined with his commitment to a more democratic form of church governance, he switched his denominational allegiance from Presbyterianism to Congregationalism.) Societally, his stress on the possibility of (qualified) human perfection and a postmillennial society reflected the positive, buoyant spirit of the country in the first half of the nineteenth century. Finney believed that Christian believers placed their spiritual lives in mortal danger if they did not cease to sin immediately. He used Enlightenment reasoning to make his point: once "light is shed upon a subject"—such as slavery or temperance—and an individual is "convinced of its iniquity," then that person "could no longer enjoy the presence of God without abandoning the sin for ever." Similarly, in his 1835 manual on how to conduct a revival, Finney was convinced that a revival could be stopped if there was "resistance to the Temperance reformation" or if "ministers and Churches take wrong ground in regard to any question involving human rights," especially slavery. Slavery

> is a subject on which [the Church] cannot be silent without guilt. . . . Shall the Church, in her efforts to reclaim and save the world, deafen her ears to this voice of agony and despair? God forbid! The Church cannot turn away from this question. It is a question for the Church and for the nation to decide, and God will push it to a decision. . . . It is in vain to account it an act of piety to turn away the ear from hearing this cry of distress.[11]

These were fighting words for men such as Thornwell, particularly when Finney backed up his words by promoting a biracial, coeducational training school for evangelists at Oberlin, Ohio.

In many ways, Finney represents the beginning of a tradition that we will explore through one hundred and fifty years—the integration of evangelical piety and progressive social concern. As we saw in the case of James Henley Thornwell, however, not all Protestants were convinced of the wisdom of this integration.

The Divided Conscience

Before we leave Finney up on a pedestal, however, it is important to see the complexity of his career, for his ministry represents the bifurcation that has plagued American Protestantism. As much as Finney was blamed during his own time, by Thornwell and others, as the initiator of rabid social engineering, and as much as he is showcased today as the forerunner of evangelical social concern, he actually had a cautious, conservative side regarding his attitude toward social problems. This attitude was evident in a number of ways. For all of his talk about temperance at the Rochester revival, for instance, he insisted that social issues were an "appendage" to the revival, not a constitutive part of his message. Although he eventually supported political efforts to extirpate slavery, he did so reluctantly, because he never wanted his politics to usurp the "great end" toward which he directed most of his efforts—"the conversion of sinners." Social questions always appear to be derivative of personal salvation.[12]

In addition, Finney believed that the United States would become righteous through the accumulated effect of millions of individuals who were converted and sanctified. He assumed that when a critical mass of the nation was born again, the purified convictions of regenerated Americans would naturally result in a purified society. It seems never to have occurred to him that there could be structural sins that demanded a social reform strategy more complex than the incremental conversion of individuals.

Furthermore, Finney articulated the Enlightenment concept of self-determining autonomy in a way that led to a rather crass reduction of the gospel message. He often referred to conversion as a simple transaction, a choosing for or against God. This "democratic" notion of God's plan of salvation fit in well with Americans' confidence in democracy and their commitment to a culture based on commodity exchange. But the fact that Finney's ideas were wedded so closely to such key American values made it difficult for him to challenge the foundational principles of the society.

Finney exemplified a progressive commitment to social action on the one hand and a rather conservative acceptance of middle-class American mores on the other. While he lifted up social issues in his preaching, he also pressed Christians to make evangelism their top priority. Historian James Moorhead refers to this dualism as the "divided conscience" of Finney and, because of his representative influence, much of American Protestantism.[13] Because of its stress on the primacy of personal decision, nineteenth-century evangelicalism was characterized by a tendency toward individualistic solutions to social problems. Yet, due to its emphasis on holiness and human progress, there was (at least in the North) a stress on the possibility of social transformation. For the followers of Finney, this resulted in a dichotomy, and his divided conscience can be traced out historically for many decades after his death—a religious dualism exacerbated by the cultural tensions of post-Civil War industrial society.

Conservative Evangelicalism

On one side, some of Finney's evangelical heirs, such as Dwight L. Moody (1837–1899), stressed his more conservative perspective, particularly his belief that the primary agent of social change was the individual. Like Finney, Moody preached that each person must become a Christian through the new birth and that social problems could be dealt with atomistically, through the personal reformation of many individuals—not institutionally or organically.

Differing from Finney, however, Moody accepted premillennialism, an eschatological doctrine that emphasized the imminent coming of Christ and the destruction of the world as we know it, prior to the establishment of the millennial reign of God on earth. Unlike Finney's optimistic postmillennialism, premillennialism was pessimistic about the role of Christians in transforming society. Premillennialists believed that the present age is corrupt. Because of the pervasive evil in the world, premillennialists felt that God's judgment was near. In the most drastic manifestations of premillennialism, the Christian's sole task is evangelism; there is no place for social restructuring because the world is simply getting worse. The thoroughgoing corruption of the present society meant that believers should have nothing to do with secular affairs.

The popularity of premillennialism among late nineteenth-century evangelicals resulted from the gradual disillusionment of many people with the social conditions of industrial America, especially among the poor and dispossessed. Christians were to separate themselves from the wicked world; the expectation of Christ's second coming and the destruction of the existing society provided hope of deliverance from the harsh realities of earthly life. Premillennialists couched their separation from sin in terms of coming out of the corruption of the "world."

One could imagine that an attack on "worldliness" could become an effective critique of bourgeois culture, and for some evangelicals of the late nineteenth and early twentieth century that was the case. In fact, William Seymour and a number of other premillennialists were active in various social concerns. More often, however, the premillennial concern to avoid worldliness took the form of a legalistic moral code, requiring Christians to separate themselves from specified personal behaviors such as drinking, dancing, playing cards, and attending theaters.

Separation of Christians from the world was often interpreted to mean that they should distance themselves from the corrupting influences of politics or secular affairs in general. In one instance, Moody responded to a group of ministers who had questioned Grover Cleveland's foreign policy.

"What right have you to criticize President Cleveland?" Moody asked. "You had better preach the gospel and let him deal with questions of state about which you know nothing."[14]

Reflecting the prevalent cultural notion of separate "spheres," Moody took for granted that males had to be involved in the ethical dilemmas inherent in the realm of business. Along with other religious leaders of the Victorian era, Moody believed that it was the appointed lot of men to encounter the moral contradictions of the world of commerce. The possible compromise of such a situation was to be mollified by the sanctifying effect of women at home and at church—carefully differentiated roles in which ethical ambiguity was the unavoidable predicament of men while self-denying purity was expected of women.

Though the conservative Protestant premillennialism of the Moody variety began in the North, the premillennial view of the Christian's limited role in the transformation of society had a deep resonance with the remnants of the "spirituality of the church" concept that had developed earlier in the South. Premillennialism, especially in an extreme form of the doctrine known as dispensationalism, neglected any systemic social reform. According to dispensationalist leader C. I. Scofield: "The best help a pastor can bring to the social problems of the community is to humble himself before God, forsake his sins, receive the filling with the Holy Spirit, and preach a pure gospel of tender love."[15] In the late nineteenth century, a connection developed between rural-oriented Northern premillennialism and the other-worldly spirituality of Southern evangelicalism—a connection that became the demographic foundation for Protestant fundamentalism.

In a sermon delivered in 1877, Moody preached that "this world is a wrecked vessel . . . God has given me a lifeboat and said, 'Moody, save all you can.'" While a "lifeboat theology" of impending divine judgement was not conducive to social change, it was a motivation to "rescue the perishing" through personal evangelism. Believers were urged to turn away from overly exclusive concerns with the world and to consider the eternal condition of their friends. Preaching the "speedy coming of Christ" became "a prominent method to lead men to repentance."[16] While for Finney, evangelism was linked to the idea that a gradual expansion of a Christianized society in this world was moving toward the postmillennial Kingdom of God, evangelism for Moody and his premillennial colleagues was linked to a culture-denying theology.

The Social Gospel

If, on the one hand, some of Finney's more conservative followers emphasized his individualism and his caution regarding social change, there were, on the other hand, some progressive followers of the evangelist who were inspired by his forceful advocacy of human rights' issues. Many people converted at Finney's revivals or educated at Oberlin were drawn toward his call for personal and social holiness. Unlike their teacher, these folks were able to move beyond Finney's anxiety that social reform would usurp the preeminent mission to evangelize souls. They emphasized the progressive possibilities of God's reign through the right willing of holy people. Also, going beyond Finney's reliance on the aggregate reformation of individuals as the only means for social change, some of Finney's revivalistic, abolitionist compatriots, realizing the interconnections between social problems such as slavery, women's rights, and the exploitation of industrial laborers, began to develop a broad-based approach to social issues. Throughout the antebellum and postbellum periods, these forerunners of the social gospel movement were able to integrate deep personal piety, a commitment to evangelism, and a passion for social transformation.

Among some Protestants in the latter years of the nineteenth century, the stress on the divine fulfillment of God's plan for this world became less identified with a cataclysmic millennial consummation of God's rule and more connected with the present Kingdom of God—a "realized eschatology." As industrialization became ever more pervasive after the Civil War, social problems—inequalities of wealth, unemployment, labor unrest, and urban poverty—became prevalent throughout the United States. The religious response was the development of the social gospel—the application of "the old message of salvation" to the entire social order.[17] The formative social gospellers, such as Washington Gladden (1836–1918) and Walter Rauschenbusch (1865–1918), were firmly grounded in nineteenth-century evangelicalism. They never saw themselves as departing from that tradition and, in terms of their positive outlook toward the progressive transformation of society that they inherited from Finney, they were correct. They regularly called themselves "evangelical liberals," a term that sounds oxymoronic to us today but seemed perfectly consistent to them.

Rauschenbusch a Baptist of German heritage, had an evangelical conversion experience of faith in Jesus Christ to which he referred often during his years of ministry. Like Charles Stelzle and some of the other social gospellers, Rauschenbusch looked up to Moody as one of his early spiritual mentors. In fact, Rauschenbusch translated the gospel choruses of Ira Sankey, Moody's song leader, into German in order that his congregation would have access to the revivalist's evangelistic worship style. Although Rauschenbusch moved on to other emphases in later years, he never deprecated his evangelical roots. He strongly advocated prayer and meditation, seeing the need for social activists "to lean back on the Eternal and to draw from the silent reservoirs." Knowing the importance of a rich and growing devotional life, he wrote *Prayers for the Social Awakening*. Even in his last and most famous book, *A Theology for the Social Gospel*, written in 1917, Rauschenbusch asserted that "the salvation of the individual is . . . an essential part of salvation." Each individual's personal commitment to Christ was "one of the miracles of life." He asked his readers to "take all the familiar experiences and truths of personal evangelism . . . for granted" in his exposition of theology, although his understanding of personal salvation was "deeply affected by the new solidaristic comprehension furnished by the social gospel."[18]

Unlike some of the later social gospellers, Rauschenbusch affirmed his support for evangelism. However, he asked an important question of traditional American evangelicalism—a question echoed later by E. Stanley Jones, Clarence Jordan, Orlando Costas, and others: "If we are converted, what are we converted to? If we are regenerated, does the scope of so divine a transformation end in our 'going to heaven'?" Rauschenbusch felt that it was time

> to overhaul our understanding of the kind of change we hope to produce by personal conversion and regeneration. . . . [S]alvation must be a change which turns a man from self to God and humanity. . . . A salvation confined to the soul and its personal interests is an imperfect and only partly effective salvation. . . . Complete salvation . . . would consist in an attitude of love in which [the believer] would freely coordinate his life with the life of his fellows in obedience to the loving impulses of the spirit of God, thus taking his part in a divine organism of mutual service.

Using language that would have been understood by mid-nineteenth century evangelicals William Goodell and Julia Foote, Rauschenbusch wrote that "[p]ersonal sanctification must serve the Kingdom of God." "A religious experience is not Christian," Rauschenbusch insisted, "unless it binds us closer to men and commits us more deeply to the Kingdom of God."[19]

The Polarization of
the Two Parties

Besides the social challenges of industrial America, other factors fomented religious division in the late nineteenth and early twentieth centuries. Along with the dichotomy that developed between evangelism and social justice there was also a theological cleavage occurring within American Protestantism. The theological controversy began with questions about the inspiration and authority of the Bible, resulting from the impact of Darwin's theory of evolution and German higher criticism, which challenged the accuracy of the scriptures. Soon, a number of traditional doctrines were being questioned. Many of those who were open to changes in the social vision of the church were also open to changes in theology.

Late nineteenth-century social Christianity began as an evangelical enterprise, but along the way some of its adherents—especially those caught up in the Biblical criticism and religious pluralism of the period—became disillusioned with orthodox evangelicalism. While Rauschenbusch and other early social gospellers were able to keep individual piety and social witness in a creative tension, not all of their successors were so adept.

Some theologians such as Shailer Mathews (1863–1941), dean of the divinity school at the University of Chicago, moved beyond the evangelical roots of Protestant liberalism and espoused a more radical "modernism." Modernists abandoned much of the traditional Christian doctrinal core while still supporting the social agenda of the Protestant churches. For Mathews, Jesus was not a personal savior but a guide and symbol for religious altruism. Among modernists, it became convenient to stress social ministry and to neglect evangelism and individual spirituality, which seemed uncritically tied to an outmoded theological system. Christ's work of personal salvation from sin, modernists frankly admitted, was "left out" of their version of religious faith. A leading liberal pastor, Harry Emerson Fosdick (1878–1969) acknowledged that many of his contemporaries could have been faulted for their "too complaisant optimism" and their "too easy surrender to current categories of modern thought."[20]

Not surprisingly, then, evangelical fervor did not remain characteristic of the later social gospel. While before, Rauschenbusch and Stelzle insisted on the unity of personal and social regeneration, later social gospellers discussed only social regeneration. The historical trajectory away from evangelical piety among the social gospellers is evident in Rauschenbusch's own family. His daughter and son-in-law became committed socialists who disregarded any association with the Christian faith, and their son (Rauschenbusch's grandson) is Richard Rorty, a renowned philosophical pragmatist who has no ties to religion.[21]

In response to the perceived threat against traditional theology and evangelism, many evangelical leaders at the turn of the twentieth century began to emphasize the need for increased attention to the Bible and the "fundamental" doctrines of the faith. Although Moody shunned controversy and was willing to work alongside almost anyone, after his death in 1899 his followers were not so irenic and helped to fan the flames of fundamentalism.

By the 1910s and 1920s, the evangelical consensus of the previous century had completely evaporated. Though both the social gospellers and the fundamentalists could rightly claim that they had roots in the evangelicalism of the previous century, by 1920 they did not want to claim any common heritage. The possibility that one could hold both a revivalistic gospel and a social gospel came to be increasingly difficult. The polarization between the social gospellers and the fundamentalists became more and more acute. Moody's heir apparent, Billy Sunday (1862–1935), gloried in his popular image as a fighting fundamentalist who had no time for social ministry. "We've had enough of this godless social service nonsense," Sunday declared when asked about his support for religious activities other than evangelism. Evangelicals who had been engaged in social action gradually pulled back from their commitments. By the 1920s, Protestants of an evangelistic and pietistic bent were almost all leaning toward conservative fundamentalism and a rejection of any transformation of social structures. Those few who continued to be involved in social ministry curtailed their activities during the Depression.

At the same time, liberalism had little tolerance for evangelical theology and its emphasis on an affective conversionist faith. In 1919, for example, the liberal magazine *Christian Century* wrote disparagingly about "the embarrassment and evils of . . . revivalism [and] traditional theology."[22] Harry Emerson Fosdick recognized and in some ways encouraged the polarization of the opposing religious camps in 1922 by publicly asking his well-heeled congregation a loaded rhetorical question: "Shall the fundamentalists win?" By framing the question in such win/lose categories, Fosdick abetted the dichotomization of the period rather than serving as an example of bridge building between the pietists and the liberal social gospellers. By the 1920s, those Protestants who were firmly committed to social change were increasingly found to have a modernist theological position. In a period when urban life was heralded as progressive and rural life was deprecated as backward, the modernists considered traditional evangelism to be irrelevant and out-of-date. They were also suspicious of any public articulation of piety.

The polarization was sharp and the suspicion deep. Conservatives thought that a stress on social action took away from the primary evangelistic mission of the church—leading people to personal faith in Christ. Meanwhile, liberals thought that a stress on individual salvation and affective piety took away from the primary transformative mission of the church—bringing God's justice to an oppressive society.

Throughout most of the nineteenth century, being an "evangelical" could and often did imply deep social concern. But beginning after the Civil War, and completed by the 1920s, an evangelistic stress on personal conversion was almost invariably linked with conservative obscurantism, while the social gospel was linked with "liberalism," "modernism," and, increasingly, with outright secularism. The two-party system of American Protestantism had become firmly demarcated and entrenched in the religious psyche.

A Holistic Vision

In the last two centuries, the main body of U.S. Protestantism has been partitioned into discrete compartments: private faith or public faith, personal piety or social action. Nevertheless, from the 1830s—when the initial inklings of a systemic approach to social problems were articulated by William Goodell and other evangelical colleagues of Charles Finney—until the present, there has been an unbroken chain of persons who have belied the division between vital piety and social transformation, who have insisted that both are necessary for a truly Christian faith. Contrary to the segmentation in much of American society, they did not separate their lives into distinct sacred and secular spheres; rather, their social justice advocacy and religious devotion were conceived of in a comprehensive way. They experienced a growing, vibrant relationship with Christ, and they interpreted that experience with an activistic theology. The result was practical social change for the sake of the reign of God on earth. In spite of cultural pressures to polarize their spirituality, they maintained a holistic vision, and thus they offer to us outstanding examples of Christian integration.

NOTES

1. Gerald R. McDermott, *One Holy and Happy Society: The Public Theology of Jonathan Edwards* (University Park, Pa: Pennsylvania State University Press, 1992), 180.

2. Charles C. Cole, *The Social Ideas of the Northern Evangelists, 1826–1860* (New York: Columbia University Press, 1954); John R. Bodo, *The Protestant Clergy and Public Issues* (Princeton, N.J.: Princeton University Press, 1954); Clifford S. Griffin, *Their Brothers' Keepers: Moral Stewardship in the United States, 1800–1865* (New Brunswick, N.J.: Rutgers University Press, 1960).

3. George M. Thomas, *Revivalism and Cultural Change: Christianity, Nation Building, and the Market in the Nineteenth-Century United States* (Chicago: University of Chicago Press, 1989); Paul E. Johnson, *A Shopkeeper's Millennium: Society and Revivals in Rochester, New York, 1815–1837* (New York: Hill & Wang, 1978).

4. For an interesting discussion of the social control thesis, see Lois W. Banner, "Religious Benevolence as Social Control: A Critique of an Interpretation," *Journal of American History* 60 (June 1973): 23–41..

5. See Robert Baird, *Religion in the United States of America. Or an Account of the Origin, Progress, Relations to the State, and Present Condition of the Evangelical Churches in the United States. With Notices of the Unevangelical Denominations* (Glasgow: Blackie & Son, 1844) and Robert Handy, *A Christian America: Protestant Hopes and Historical Realities*, 2d ed. (New York: Oxford University Press, 1984).

6. Jay Dolan, *Catholic Revivalism: The American Experience, 1830–1900* (South Bend, In.: University of Notre Dame Press, 1978).

7. Cited in Martin E. Marty, *Righteous Empire: The Protestant Experience in America* (New York: Dial Press, 1970), 118.

8. Ernest Trice Thompson, *The Spirituality of the Church: A Distinctive Doctrine of the Presbyterian Church in the United States* (Richmond: John Knox Press, 1961), 21.

9. Ibid., 23–25.

10. Whitney R. Cross, *The Burned-Over District: The Social and Intellectual History of Enthusiastic Religion in Western New York, 1800–1850* (Ithaca, N.Y.: Cornell University Press, 1950).

11. Charles G. Finney, *Lectures on Revivals of Religion* (New York: Fleming H. Revell Co., 1868), 272–73.

12. *Oberlin Evangelist* (24 September 1845): 155.

13. James M. Moorhead, "Social Reform and the Divided Conscience of Antebellum Protestantism," *Church History* 48 (December 1979): 416–30.

14. *Boston Evening Transcript* (7 January 1897), cited in James F. Findlay Jr., *Dwight L. Moody: American Evangelist, 1837–1899* (Chicago: University of Chicago Press, 1969), 277.

15. Cited in George M. Marsden, *Fundamentalism and American Culture: The Shaping of Twentieth-Century Evangelicalism* (New York: Oxford University Press, 1980), 255n.

16. *New York Evangelist* 46 (19 August 1875): 6.

17. Walter Rauschenbusch, *A Theology for the Social Gospel* (Nashville: Abingdon Press, 1978; original publication date, 1917), 5.

18. Ibid., 95–96.

19. Ibid., 100, 105.

20. William R. Hutchison, *The Modernist Impulse in American Protestantism* (Oxford: Oxford Univesity Press, 1976); Harry Emerson Fosdick, *The Living of These Days: An Autobiography* (New York: Harper Brothers, 1956), 66.

21. Robert Hollinger and David Depew, eds., *Pragmatism: From Progressivism to Postmodernism* (Westport, Conn.: Praeger Publishers, 1995), 47–48.

22. Cited in Marsden, 166.

1.

WILLIAM GOODELL
(1792–1878)

Antislavery Church Reformer and Politician:
Making Progress in Holy Activity

D espite the fact that they may have had an important influence on American religious life, some historical figures are not well-known today simply because of oversight on the part of historians. This neglect has been recognized recently (and to some degree corrected) in regard to women and people of color, whose contributions were often disregarded by scholars. Other significant people have not received recognition due to the cumulative effect of historians' decisions to identify someone else as representative of a particular movement or idea. William Goodell is such an overlooked person—one who, similar to many of the individuals in this volume, has become an obscure figure in the religious history of the United States.

The continued obscurity of Goodell's life and witness is to our detriment. Though a leading antislavery advocate and a model of the sort of Christian integration highlighted in this book, Goodell's reputation suffered because he happened to be opposed to the views of William Lloyd Garrison, the best-known American abolitionist. Historians have generally followed Garrison's interpretation of events, and thus the perspective of Goodell and his fellow "political abolitionists" is often ignored or unfairly characterized.

Goodell's vision is important for us to retrieve, for he was an exemplar and one of the earliest promoters of what he called "a whole gospel." The whole gospel, according to Goodell, was a rich and growing Christian spirituality that began with a new birth experience, continued to "make progress" in a sanctified life, and resulted in a lifetime of "holy activity." This last concept was an aspect of Goodell's spirituality that was relatively new in American Protestantism, a strategic shift that moved evangelical social thought toward (what would later become known as) the social gospel. By "holy activity," Goodell was not simply referring to a life of sanctified ethical action (although his conception included that); he also meant a process of spiritual growth in which Christians recognized the need to address social problems by systemic means as well as by individual conversion.[1]

"A High Type of Piety and an Enlarged Benevolence"

Goodell spent his earliest years in the same "burned-over" environment of upstate New York that spawned Charles Finney. There on the New York frontier, the young Goodell attended a Methodist class meeting with his parents. A childhood illness that left him bedridden for two years led to a lifelong interest in reading and writing. He devoured the Bible, *Pilgrim's Progress,* and the writings of John Wesley, all of which encouraged him to live out an activistic faith. Orphaned at the age of fourteen, Goodell went to live with his grandmother in Connecticut. She was a devout Congregationalist who had heard Jonathan Edwards preach and had been converted under the ministry of the famous evangelist George Whitefield. She was also firmly committed to the principles of the American Revolution. Thus, early on, Goodell was imbued with the ideals of both evangelical piety and democratic liberty.[2]

In 1830 Goodell attended the famous Rochester revival that brought Finney to national attention. Thereafter, the two men followed similar paths as evangelical reformers. In fact, it was perhaps due to Finney's influence that, several years later, Goodell became a strong promoter of the experience of sanctification. That is, Goodell's theological formulation went beyond the standard evangelical profession of a "new birth" conversion to include the concept of Christian perfection. He became convinced that it was essential for the "new heart" in Christ to be "evinced by a holy life." Goodell still believed in the necessity of regenerative conversion, but now he insisted that "souls are truly converted" only when their sins, both personal and social, were abandoned. The goal of the Christian believer was "to be wholly sanctified," which, he concluded, was "to be wholly free from sin." Consistent with the beliefs of other nineteenth-century evangelical perfectionists, Goodell did not believe in absolute human perfection. Rather, he affirmed that Christians could, through God's grace, conform their will to the divine will in such a way that their ethical behavior reflected God's standard of equality for all persons. Goodell advocated, as he put it, both "a high type of piety [affective evangelical experience] and an enlarged benevolence [ever-increasing activism]."[3]

Goodell expressed his "high type of piety" in a religious faith that was vital, affective, and actively cultivated. "Daily communion with the Spirit," he was convinced, would help each believer to become "more and more intimately acquainted with Christ." Goodell's daughter, Maria, remembered that family devotions "were full of life and earnestness, never degenerating into a mere form, and always constituted an important feature in daily life."[4]

Goodell insisted that Christianity "is an every day business, and has something to do with everything with which [people] have any thing to do."[5] One area in which holiness was to be clearly evident was in a person's lifestyle. He carefully disciplined his daily routine, including the things that he ate and drank. Goodell also hoped to set an example as a parent. His daughter remembered how he strove to inculcate moral values in his children. "Material wants held a subordinate place" in their home, for example, and he ingrained in his children the basic principles of human equality. In order to remind his daughters of their moral responsibility to the oppressed, Goodell placed the picture of an African American girl on their work bags, needle books, and pin cushions, along with the words: "Am I not a woman and a sister?" Dinner was served on plates inscribed with appropriate quotations from the Declaration of Independence and the Bible, particularly the text "Of one blood are all nations of men" (Acts 17:26). His daughter long remembered the lessons of those years: "When I sat down to dinner every day, literally with my child's bowl of bread and milk I drank in also the question of equal rights."[6]

Faith, Goodell believed, was to be lived out in daily life, especially in moral purity and in relationships with others. He regularly opened his home to indigent people, including many fugitive slaves. He believed that a true Christian must apply the principles of Jesus in his or her personal life and there must be a congruence between one's confession of Christ and one's character, a unity of profession and practice. He rejected the argument that "the supposed piety of the inward act . . . compensates for the profligacy of the outward act"—that is, that deeply felt religious emotion could make up for a person's ethical lapses. He also rejected the opposite contention—that social justice advocacy made piety and personal moral behavior superfluous. Goodell argued against those who isolated Christian faith by making it applicable in only one aspect of life, either individual or corporate. Religion was a continual experience and a thoroughgoing obligation, to be applied to both private and public acts. Goodell knew from his own experience that a "high type of piety" was crucial for his spiritual well-being, but he was also convinced that the personal piety of Christians needed to be matched by an "enlarged benevolence" toward humanity.

Like most nineteenth-century Americans, Goodell was a child of the Enlightenment. He believed that objective truth was discernible as long as persons had the opportunity for free investigation and enough education to understand the truth once they were exposed to it. It was every believer's duty to "make progress," that is, to act on the knowledge that one had gained. Holiness was not complex or unfathomable; in fact, once a thorough understanding of God's will was ascertained, there was a certain "simplicity" to the moral actions expected of Christians. "The more the Christian learns of God and divine truth," Goodell believed, "the more he will love them and become conformed to them." As people's minds were opened to new understandings about God and neighbor, they would want to change their behavior to be in conformity with the new knowledge. In the words of Goodell's contemporary James Russell Lowell: "new occasions teach new duties." The Christian, according to Goodell,

> sees more and more . . . the degradation of his species, the brutality of the sensual, the oppression of the wronged, the cruelty of the oppressor, the sorrows of the oppressed. . . . And in all of this, the Christian sees, more and more, of the work for God and for humanity, that needs to be done, and he feels more and more the weight of obligation resting on him to do with his might what his hands find to do, in this vast field of his labor.[7]

Political Abolitionism

Convinced of the need to lead an activist Christian life, Goodell did "with his might what his hands f[ou]nd to do." He used his writing abilities to develop a career as a religious journalist editing reform-oriented, weekly newspapers. Initially, he crusaded against the evils of liquor. He never dropped his interest in curbing the consumption of alcohol, but by 1833 his close friend William Lloyd Garrison persuaded him to put his greatest energies into the antislavery struggle. Goodell helped Garrison organize the American Anti-Slavery Society and was named as the first editor of the Society's newspaper, the *Emancipator*. In this role, Goodell was one of the first abolitionists to use the Declaration of Independence and the Constitution to argue that the antislavery cause was connected logically to the broader issue of obtaining civil liberties for African Americans.

During the late 1830s and early 1840s, Goodell and a number of other leading abolitionists became impatient with Garrison's tactic of "moral suasion," a strategic measure by which reformers persuaded others one by one that slavery was sinful. Goodell was convinced that it was necessary to work for abolition through the legislative process as well as through the incremental conversion of individuals. By 1837 he became the leading spokesperson for these "political abolitionists."

Their strategy was to form a new, explicitly Christian, antislavery political party. The "Liberty Party," as they called it, was to be a moral alternative to the unprincipled compromising with slaveholders that characterized the two major parties, the Whigs and the Democrats. Goodell and the original members of the party were evangelical perfectionists who desired to express their holiness through politics. In fact, Goodell introduced a new theological innovation into nineteenth-century evangelicalism: he contended that the spiritual commitment of sanctification was directly connected to one's political actions. He was critical of any constructions of evangelical theology that did not include specific social reform activity, and he defined obedience to God's law in a way that insisted on each sanctified person's involvement in political abolition. Goodell stated that sanctification, if properly understood, would result in the righteous fulfillment of "political duties." "The Liberty Party was born," said the political abolitionists, "to demonstrate the maxim that religion has everything to do with politics."[8]

When Goodell and his colleagues embraced this unequivocal political strategy, it indicated a new beginning for evangelicals in the United States; in effect, modern social Christianity was born. Typically, it has been argued that a structural analysis of social problems did not begin among Christians in the United States until Washington Gladden and other social gospellers addressed the challenge of industrial conditions in the years following the Civil War. But as early as the antebellum period, Goodell and other political abolitionists began to comprehend the interconnectedness of various corporate sins in American society and the need to address these problems structurally. Ever since the late 1830s—in one form or another—American Protestants have been directly engaged in the public sphere in terms of a systemic strategy of organized action.

This period in the late 1830s also marked the beginning of Goodell's estrangement from his two mentors, Garrison and Finney. A profound ideological difference caused the separation between Goodell and Garrison. As Garrison struggled against the coercive institution of slavery, he came to believe that all humanly organized institutions were inherently corrupt—including governments, since they relied on the force of law to back up their authority. He regarded political action of any kind, even voting for the abolition of slavery, as accommodating with demonic institutional forces. Garrison determined that abolitionists should avoid associating with political parties because, by their very nature, they implicitly supported the governmental structure of the United States. Since, according to Garrison, partisan activity lowered the abolitionist movement into the "dirty waters of politics," then Liberty Party members were traitors to the antislavery cause. In his anger, he painted political abolitionists with one broad brush stroke. Garrison—and later historians, who have tended to rely on Garrison's rendering—lumped all political abolitionists, Goodell included, into one category as partisan opportunists who compromised the integrity of the antislavery movement.

Unlike Garrison, Finney had no moral qualms about the political involvement of Christians, and, in fact, he publicly supported the Liberty Party. The great revivalist, however, was concerned that too much political activity diminished the evangelistic resources available for the church's primary task of converting the unregenerate. In this matter, Finney echoed a common fear of evangelical ministers. In one such instance, a preacher worried that the attendance of his congregants at too many political conventions would "reduce the spirituality and religious feeling of his flock." Goodell became exasperated with Finney and other "clerical pretenders to a holiness that cannot preach politics—that cannot mingle with politics."[9]

Along with the criticisms of his two erstwhile friends, Goodell also had to contend with the opposition of officials from the leading denominations and the traditional political parties. They were convinced that theological beliefs and party platforms belonged within entirely separate "spheres" of life. The leaders of religious and civil institutions alike asserted that there was to be a clear division between the expression of one's religious faith and one's activity in the affairs of government. Religious practice and partisan politics had definite, prescribed boundaries. The politicians were fearful of clerical domination in the civil government. The denominational leaders believed that Christianity should concentrate on "spiritual" things and not get tangled up in political wrangling. Partisan activity was considered improper for church members, especially when they were operating within their official ecclesiastical capacities.

Goodell believed that this was an arbitrary dichotomy. He responded that there could be no such division for the sanctified Christian, and he challenged the prevailing notion of separate spheres. He did so because he resented the reduced status that was ascribed to the religious sphere in such a scheme. Why, he queried, should not persons of moral conviction be a conscious part of the political process? If ethical values were not involved in the political process, Goodell argued, then it might as well be admitted that the government had no moral foundation and was capable of nothing but corruption. (For Goodell's argument on this score, see the selection from his article "Religion and Politics" at the end of this chapter.)

What if, he argued, religious reformers like himself expanded the strategies that were traditionally considered acceptable for evangelical benevolence (such as evangelism and education) to incorporate political action? Then they could raise the moral tone of the political culture in the United States. Indeed, Liberty Party members were convinced that the entire democratic process in America could be purified. Goodell was not advocating the union of church and state. He was against any "enforcement of a religious creed, or form of worship, by the secular arm." However, he did believe in the influence of "true religion—of just views and an honest regard of human rights, human relations, human duties, and moral obligations, over the political transactions of men."[10]

Democratizing Church Government

Goodell's vision of the comprehensiveness of Christ's call to a holy life also compelled him to extend his reform interests in other ways, beyond the justification of political action among religious reformers. The concept of "abolitionism" came to mean more for him than just antislavery. According to the religious reasoning of the political abolitionists, the abolition of chattel slavery was simply a first step in the "immediate abolition of iniquity" required in one's personal life and in the nation.[11] Slavery became a paradigm for tyrannical institutions that existed throughout the society. In particular, Goodell compared the legal despotism enslaving African Americans to the "spiritual despotism" enslaving evangelical Americans. "Despotic power in the church, in the state, and on the plantation, are one and the same in nature, though differing in degree, and all alike are forbidden by Jesus Christ"—for all claimed "exclusive, unlimited power" over other people.[12] The fact that the major denominations and political parties refused to condemn slaveholders was simply a specific example of the fetters that such institutions imposed generally upon the human conscience.

This "ecclesiastical slavery," according to Goodell and his colleagues, was vividly demonstrated by the prescribed dogma and authoritative judicatories of the denominations. In the opinion of these reformers, "the chains" of hierarchical denominations "bind the souls of God's children as the chains of Southern tyrants bind the bodies of men." Large, national religious institutions were considered inherently sinful—especially denominations with a connectional polity, such as Presbyterianism and Methodism. God's millennial government could not be established through the instrumentality of these faulty human constructs.[13]

Because of the continued support of slavery among U.S. denominations, Goodell stated that "the prevalent . . . religion of America . . . is not Christianity, but its impudent counterfeit." Anticipating an argument made today by liberation theologians, Goodell declared that "sound" religion could exist within "corrupt" nations such as the United States only "among the minority, among those who hold not the power . . . among the victims." Since traditional denominations were considered unredeemably sinful, the recourse for Christians seeking to live a holy life was to "separate from the prominent religious sects of this country." The "spiritual despotism" of old, impure denominations was to be replaced with the "spiritual democracy" of reorganized, purified congregations. Goodell was so committed to this vision of a spiritual democracy that he established and for ten years served as the unordained pastor of an "Independent Abolition Church" in Honeoye, New York.[14]

Structural Sin
and Social Redemption

Along with his efforts to democratize church government, another example of Goodell's desire to "make progress in holy activity" was his work
to expand the political agenda of the Liberty Party. By the late 1840s, the
Liberty Party was beginning to attract a larger cross section of northern
voters, many of whom, predictably, were not as religiously motivated as
Goodell and the original political abolitionist leadership. Some Liberty
members joined the party for their own political self-aggrandizement. Others liked the Liberty Party because they wanted to oppose the South and to
promote the interests of Northern white "free labor." Often they were not
in favor of increasing the civil rights of African Americans, and some were
not even opposed to slavery. New leaders assumed control of the party apparatus, and they believed that the moral vision and religious trappings of
the original party leadership were a hindrance to political success. They
suggested that the Liberty Party merge with disaffected Whigs and Democrats into a secular party configuration, initially called the Free Soil Party.
(Later, through another party reorganization, this group became part of the
new Republican Party.)

Goodell vehemently opposed the political merger. Instead, he projected
an expanded and more ambitious platform for the Liberty Party that would
increase its moral engagement rather than diminish it. Just as he challenged
the narrow sphere of personal morality that had traditionally been considered to be the only appropriate arena of service for religiously motivated
people, he now challenged other notions of limited spheres operating
within U.S. society. Many people were forced into restricted roles due to
their ethnicity, gender, or economic status. Goodell repudiated these "artificial" distinctions and championed equal rights for various oppressed
groups: African Americans, Mexican Americans, Native Americans, Chinese Americans, industrial workers, and women. He and other Liberty
Party leaders, for instance, encouraged women and African Americans to
take positions of party leadership and nominated them for public office—
the first time in American history that persons from these groups were provided the opportunity to exercise political power.

Goodell pushed the Liberty Party to deal with all of these equal rights
concerns—not diminishing the importance of slavery but adding other issues that also needed urgent attention. Any "fragmentary policy of reformation is decidedly anti-evangelical . . . in its tendency," he stated. Since
evangelicals believed in the sinful corruption of all humanity, then Goodell
assumed that "each specific vice is only a particular form or manifestation of
a general disease." "All fragmentary reformations," he was convinced,
"strike only at . . . one of what the evangelical philosophy [theology] treats

as branches, without laying the axe, as that philosophy teaches us to do, at the root of the tree." Social evils were to be removed at their root—the sinful structures that existed both within individual lives and within the "abuses [that] are inherent in the system." Goodell spoke often about the "forms of oppression that cluster around [slavery] and support it." "Wrongs are so mutually sustaining, and so much parts of one whole," the 1848 Liberty Party convention declared, "as to require the war to be against all of them, in order to be successful against any of them."[15]

Understanding the unified character of sin led Goodell to understand the need for a unified solution to destroy it. He came to view his "one-idea" of abolishing slavery as an "isolated, partial, specific opposition to particular forms and instances of oppression" that ought to be "displaced by the all-comprehensive, generalized idea of opposition to ALL oppression."[16] By the late 1840s, Goodell and other political abolitionists were leading the way in the transition from the emphasis on individualized redemption characteristic of the revivalistic period to an emphasis on the combination of individual redemption with social redemption characteristic of the early social gospel era.

Goodell called for both the sanctification of individuals and the sanctification of structures in order to perfect the society. As an evangelical, he did not want to neglect the "old remedy of regenerating the man individually, before he can be regenerated socially." But Goodell continued his appeal in more solidaristic terms:

> Along with this old truth we must not take the old error that too commonly went with it, the error of forgetting that man individually, is a social being, with a moral nature socially defined, with social relations binding him in every direction, with social responsibilities intertwined with every fibre of his being, with social duties pressing every where upon him, as the condition of his individual existence and well being. To regenerate the man individually, he must be regenerated in his social affections and habits.[17]

For Goodell, personal and social redemption fit like hand and glove.

Although the voting constituency of the Liberty Party became negligible after 1848, Goodell maintained his political convictions—almost singlehandedly—until the start of the Civil War. In 1852, the few remaining Liberty Party members reorganized themselves as the Radical Abolition Party, and Goodell accepted nomination as their presidential candidate. He knew that he had no real chance of electoral victory, but he saw his role as a goad to further "progress in holy activity."

With the arrival of the War, Goodell—now an old man—tried to influence the political rhetoric of the North. Twice he made personal visits to

Lincoln at the White House to press his point. The war should not be justified as a sectional conflict to preserve the union, he asserted, but as a "second American Revolution" that was necessary to finish the democratic task left uncompleted by the first Revolution, particularly in terms of race. As we read the following selections from Goodell's writings regarding the Christian's obligation to live a holy life and the proper role of religion in the public square, it is easy to see how his prophetic words were appropriate not only for his own time but for ours as well.

Selections From the
Writings of William Goodell

from "Christian Progress," (1848)[18]

The Christian is making progress in the knowledge of God, his Creator and Father; of Jesus Christ, his Mediator and Redeemer; of the Holy Spirit his Sanctifier, his Comforter, and his Teacher. As he walks with God daily, he is making daily advances in his acquaintance with him. As he leans constantly on Christ, his wisdom, his righteousness, his sanctification, his redemption, he cannot help becoming more and more intimately acquainted with Christ, the friend that sticketh closer than a brother. As his spirit holds daily communion with the Spirit of all grace and consolation, he necessarily becomes more familiarized with his refreshings and his teachings. . . .

The Christian is making progress in holiness. . . . The more the Christian learns of God and divine truth, the more he will love them and become conformed to them, in heart and life, which is the same thing as increasing in holiness.—On the other hand, the more the Christian loves God and divine truth, and the more he walks in conformity with them, the more he will *desire* to learn, and consequently, *will* learn of them. . . .

[I]t is only in the exercise of holy love and in the filial discharge of the duties growing out of our heaven-appointed relations, and the immutable nature of things that the glory and beauty of those sublime doctrines by which moral objects are described and human relations revealed, are healthfully and clearly perceived. . . .

As the Christian prays for increasing light and love, for larger measures of wisdom and knowledge, of holiness and conformity to God, and as he uses the divinely appointed means of their attainment; wrestling, struggling, running, fighting, agonizing, to reach the object he has in view, the prize he is panting after, so, of course, he is making advances towards the glorious goal of his destiny. He is becoming more god-like, more stable, more constant in the exercise of holy affections. He is less frequently turned aside—less easily overcome by temptation. With each increase of divine knowledge his soul expands and becomes more capacious. With each expansion he still loves God with all his heart and soul, and mind and strength, and consequently his holy love is increased. Each increase of holy love, in its turn, lets in a new flood of divine light, with which, again his capacities expand. . . .

The Christian is making progress in holy activity, in benevolent self denial, in patient labor, in Christian enterprize, in solid usefulness.

This results, of necessity, from his progress in knowledge and holiness, in the love of God and of mankind. . . .

To love God is to serve God. To love man is to do good to man. Holiness is another name for benevolence, or love: for "love is the fulfilling of the law." Love is the essence of the gospel. . . .

To increase in holiness is to increase in love, in practical, matter-of-fact goodness, benevolence, justice, equity, mercy, towards men; and in obedience, fidelity, humility, submission, veneration, towards God.

As the Christian learns more of God and of man—and as he loves God and man more and more, he becomes more and more interested for the glory of God and the well being of man: he becomes more and more engaged in the service of God, and mankind. . . .

The more he learns of Christian truth and duty, of the commandments of God, of the principles and aims which mould and shape all divine institutions, and all divinely appointed relations, the more, of course, he discovers prevailing departures from the spirit of those institutions, the demands of those relations, and of the guilt and misery involved in those departures. He learns more of the necessity of numerous enterprises of amelioration and of philanthropy, of efforts for reformation, in the Church, in the State, in the community to which he belongs, and throughout the world. He sees more dearly and feels more deeply, the moral darkness and corruption of a world lying in wickedness, the wants and the woes of crushed and bleeding humanity, the guilt, the wretchedness, and the danger of lost sinners, of the heathen abroad. . . . He sees more and more . . . the degradation of his species, the brutality of the sensual, the oppression of the wronged, the cruelty of the oppressor, the sorrows of the oppressed. . . .

And in all of this, the Christian sees, more and more, of the work for God and for humanity, that needs to be done, and he feels more and more the weight of obligation resting on him to do with his might what his hands find to do, in this vast field of his labor.

The more progress the Christian makes in practical experience, in wisdom, in knowledge, in holiness, in conformity to God, the more enterprising, and active, and self denying, and uncompromising does he become, in every enterprize of philanthropy and Christian reformation, in every evangelizing and missionary endeavor—in suitable measures for calling sinners to repentance, for instructing and comforting Christians, for restoring and sustaining the holy order of Christ's house, and for bringing the kingdoms of this world under the dominion of the Prince of Peace.

The more he becomes acquainted with the extent of the divine requirements, the fraternity of the Christian virtues, the confederacy between all the powers of darkness, the unity and comprehensiveness of the divine aims, the universal applicability of the first principles which, in the beginning of his labors he had learned to apply in only a few obvious directions; the more in the progress of his labors he finds occasion and necessity for the wider and still wider application of these same principles, the more will the Christian, in the very act of making progress, come into sympathy and co-operation with the comprehensiveness and unity of the divine aims. His plans and his enterprizes will be enlarged. He will raise higher and still higher, in the name of his Master, his divine claims. He will find his work to be no fragmentary work. He will wage an uncompromising warfare with all sin. . . .

One reformatory, benevolent, or evangelizing enterprise, whether completed or in progress, is only the Christian laborer's stepping stone to another, and yet another, and never will he be content to cease his refor-· matory labor, while life lasts, unless he can see every sin overthrown, and the whole earth filled with the knowledge, the love, and the glory of God, as the waters cover the sea.

from "Religion and Politics—The Relation Between the Church and the
   State," (1843)[19]

Not a step can be taken by good men towards rebuking wickedness in high places, and especially in the direction of wielding their own powers and honoring their own responsibilities, as citizens, in the election of good rulers, and breaking the yoke of oppression—without rousing against them the clamors of the thoughtless and the designing, who, with one loud voice, vociferate, "CHURCH AND STATE! CHURCH AND STATE!" . . .

It is in consequence, partly, of these clamors that many ministers decline espousing the cause of the oppressed. It is regarded as a *political* question; and with *politics,* they have been led to conclude, the clergy must not interfere. Whenever satan can contrive to get any sin sanctioned by the laws of the *State,* that sin is, henceforth, beyond the reach of clerical rebuke, because the clergy must let political questions alone! . . .

Another delusion results, of necessity, from the preceding. When the laws of God—in other words, the great principles of eternal *right* (the principles upon which human nature is constructed, and God's providential government is administered)—have ceased to be urged upon men wielding civil power—when those principles no longer control men in their political actions—when statutes are enacted, and legislators elected, and when public business of all sorts is conducted, on the assumption that morality and religion have nothing to do with politics, and that God takes no cognizance of men's political conduct—*what is the result?* What *can* it be, but that human selfishness reigns unchecked; that falsehood and deceit, that violence and fraud, that injustice and oppression, pervade every department of political life? *Politics become corrupt,* and men cease to *expect* anything but corruption in political men. And since politics are thus corrupt and corrupting, the *minister of religion* (through whose guilty neglect the corruption of politics has become thus proverbial) finds a *fresh reason* why *he* should not meddle with politics! The contact might endanger the purity of his reputation—detract from the dignity of his profession—reduce the amount of his influence—disturb the quiet of his meditations, and lower the standard of his spirituality and religious feeling! And thus his previous habit of neglecting to teach the political duties and reprove the political iniquities of men is strengthened and confirmed.

The next result is, that the deacon and the lay elder, as well as the minister, begin to talk of the "dirty waters of politics. . . ."

And hence the pathetic exhortations so often addressed to the friends of temperance and of the enslaved, not to degrade and sully their benevolent and holy enterprise by dragging it down into "the dirty waters of politics!" And these exhortations commonly come from those who are *themselves* chin-deep in those same "dirty waters"—from those whose disregard of fundamental morality, in their political activities, were sufficient to make political waters dirty. . . .

If politics be too polluting for the minister, then they are too polluting for the deacon—too polluting for the Christian—too polluting for any one who intends to *be* a Christian. . . .

The harsh bearing of all this, upon reformatory efforts, whether in the Church or in the State, must be apparent to men of observation and refection. "It is a moral question," says one, "do not pollute it with politics." "It is a political question," says another, "do not pollute the churches with it." Just as though a moral question could have no political bearings! Just as though political questions could involve no moral principles!

How can the State be reformed without any reference to the moral principles by which the State should be governed? Or how shall we conceive of a reform in the Churches which shall leave their members in the practice of all manner of iniquity in their relations to the State? How shall we conceive of the abolition of slavery, without a repeal of the slave laws? Or how shall laws be repealed without political action of some sort, either in the judiciary, in the legislature, or at the ballot-box?

To say that politics—that legislation must not be employed against any moral evils, is to say that we must have no penal code—no laws against murder or theft, or against any invasion of human rights—in other words, that there should be no civil government at all!

Or, on the other hand, to say that the churches and ministry must reprove no crimes that are to be repressed by legislation, is to say they must not reprove murder or arson, adultery or theft. . . .

To commend one statesman as honest, and to condemn another as perfidious, becomes worse than unmeaning, more unintelligible than jargon, unless morality and religion hold rightful authority in the department of politics. An end to all political obligation follows, of course. Whenever we use the words *ought,* or *ought not,* whenever we apply the terms *right* and *wrong* to any political conduct, our words, if they mean anything, mean that men are *morally accountable* for their *political conduct.* . . .

Who does not know that, as a matter of fact and a matter of necessity, the religion of every nation under heaven gives shape and character to its political institutions? Where do you find the security of human rights and the enjoyment of civil and religious freedom, to any degree or extent, except among a people who, to the same degree and extent, recognize a religion that defines human rights, and prohibits aggressions upon them? . . .

It is the actually prevalent religion—the practical, not the professed nor the theoretical, religion of a country that controls it. The prevalent, the dominant religion of . . . America is *not* Christianity, but its impudent counterfeit. . . . [T]he *actual* religion of the Slave States—nay, of the U[nited] States—the prevalent, the controlling religion of this country, is fairly expressed in the bloody pages of the slave code! And those who mean to have and maintain a different religion, must separate from the prominent religious sects of this country.

When we say "the prevalent," "the controlling" religion of a country, we mean to recognize the fact that a sound religion may exist—in countries politically despotic and corrupt—exist among the minority, among those who hold not the power—exist among the victims, and not among the perpetrators of political rapacity. What we mean to affirm is, that every nation *has* its prevailing, its controlling religion—the religion of those who govern the State; and that the moral character of this religion decides of necessity, and invariably, the political character of the government. And we say, too, that the obviousness of this fact stamps with shallowness, not to say lunacy, the idle prattle that "religion has nothing to do, or *ought* to have nothing to do, with politics!" . . . Religion (good or bad religion) consists in action—moral action—social action. . . .

What is it, then, that we are to regard as an iniquitous and mischievous union of Church and State? The establishment, by law, of a national, or State religion, is the evil to be deprecated, is it not? [It is] the enforcement of a religious creed, or form of worship, by the secular arm.

. . . What *is* the union of which wise and good men should be afraid? Is it the natural, the healthful, the necessary control of true religion—of just views and an honest regard of human rights, human relations, human duties, and moral obligations, over the political transactions of men? Certainly not. For this, and nothing else, can *secure* civil and religious freedom.

NOTES

1. *Christian Investigator* 6 (April 1848): 496; 6 (May 1848): 500.

2. See M. Leon Perkal, "William Goodell: A Life of Reform" (Ph.D. diss., City University of New York, 1972).

3. Many of the manuscript sermons in the Goodell papers at Berea College are about entire sanctification, holiness, or Christian perfection: "Wesley's Plain Account of Christian Perfection," "Discussions on Perfection," "Entire Sanctification," "Relation of Holiness to Happiness."

4. *Christian Investigator* 6 (May 1848): 500; Maria G. Frost, "Life of Lavinia Goodell," Goodell papers, Berea College, Berea, Ky.

5. *Christian Investigator* (January 1, 1841).

6. Ibid.

7. *Christian Investigator* 6 (May 1848): 500.

8. Goodell, "Entire Sanctification," "Discussion on Perfection," 14 Goodell Paper Berea College; *The Liberty Press* 4 (13 December 1845): 21. See also *Christian Investigator* 1 (June 1843): 47–48; (September 1843): 60; 2 (July 1844): 149. For a further description of the connection between evangelicalism and the Liberty Party, see Douglas M. Strong, "The Application of Perfectionism to Politics: Political and Ecclesiastical Abolitionism in the Burned-Over District," *Wesleyan Theological Journal* 25, no. 1 (spring 1990): 21–41.

9. *Christian Investigator* 1 (September 1843): 59; Goodell, "Discussions on Perfection," 14, Goodell papers, Berea College.

10. *Christian Investigator* 1 (September 1843): 61.

11. Jonathan Blanchard, *A Perfect State of Society* (Oberlin, Ohio: James Steele, 1839), 12.

12. *Christian Investigator* 4 (October 1846): 366.

13. *The Christian Union* 1 (August 1841): 61; *Christian Investigator* 1 (May 1843): 31; 1 (July 1843): 42.

14. *Christian Investigator* 1 (September 1843): 57–61.

15. *Christian Investigator* 6 (April 1848): 496; 4 (October 1846): 366; Liberty Party, *Proceedings of the National Liberty Convention, Held at Buffalo, N.Y., June 14th and 15th, 1848* (Utica, N.Y.: S.W. Green), 30; William Goodell, *Address of the Macedon Convention By William Goodell* (Albany, N.Y.: S.W. Green, Patriot Office, 1847), 6–8.

16. Goodell, *Address of the Macedon Convention*, 10.

17. *Christian Investigator* 5 (November 1847): 458; 6 (April 1848): 496; 6 (June 1848): 507–8.

18. William Goodell, "Christian Progress," *Christian Investigator* 6 (May 1848): 500–501.

19. William Goodell, "Religion and Politics—The Relation Between the Church and the State," *Christian Investigator* 1 (September 1843): 57–61.

2.

JULIA A. J. FOOTE
(1823–1900)
Holiness Preacher:
Overcoming Prejudice Through Sanctification

Though Julia Foote was born "free" in Schenectady, New York, in 1823, she grew up in a social climate of unremitting racism. As a woman of color, she carried the double burden of racial and gender discrimination. Foote fought against these cultural barriers throughout her life. Like many black women today, her attack upon prescribed social boundaries was stubborn, determined, and sometimes even ornery. Foote's unshakable perseverance in the face of oppression has earned her and other nineteenth century African American women preachers a place of honor among contemporary womanist[1] scholars.

What is missing, however, from many of the recent portrayals of nineteenth century African American women is a nuanced understanding of the specific religious commitments that provided the foundation for their bold behavior. The distinctive beliefs that motivated them have been neglected. This is unfortunate, for according to Foote's own account, it was the theological substance of her Christian faith that was the most essential feature of who she was as a person. In order to appreciate the full measure of Julia Foote's personal journey, it is fundamental that we rediscover and celebrate her inner life of the Spirit as well as her impressive and courageous outward actions.

Foote understood her spirituality to be interrelated with her vocational purpose. For over fifty years, her single-minded mission was "to testify . . . to the sufficiency of the blood of Jesus Christ to save from all sin." That is, she wanted Christians—and especially those of her "own race"—to receive the "second blessing" of entire sanctification, an experience that she herself obtained after her evangelical conversion. Foote described sanctification as "a second, distinct work of the Holy Ghost" that followed upon one's regenerative new birth in Christ. She and other so-called "Holiness" preachers believed that the experience of sanctification gave rise to a higher degree of consecrated living for God. Foote provided clear and unequivocal reasoning for her determined advocacy of the doctrine and experience of holiness. According to her understanding, once sanctified, the spiritual life of Christians would be more consistent and resolute. She was convinced that the "immovable" faith commitment resulting from sanctification allowed believers to overcome any prejudice they might face—whether on account of their race, sex, vocational call, or theological viewpoint.[2]

The historical record of many nineteenth-century black women is sparse, and available materials on the life of Julia Foote are rather limited. We do not even know her given surname, for instance; "Foote" was her husband's last name. Most of the information about her comes from her autobiography, *A Brand Plucked From the Fire*.[3] Thomas K. Doty, the editor who wrote the introduction to Foote's book, described her biographical record as "a simple narrative of a life of incidents, many of them stirring and strange."[4] Doty was correct—Foote's narrative is simple, stirring, and, to our minds, perhaps even strange. But it is also profound. For Julia Foote's life story offers an account of deep spiritual grounding—a description of a vital, growing Christian commitment that gave her the strength to strive against the multiform oppressions of her day.

Indignities and Affirmations

Key to comprehending Foote's narrative is an understanding of the word "prejudice," a term she employed frequently. We often use the word to designate an attitude of hostility directed toward persons of another race or ethnicity. While Foote sometimes understood prejudice in that particular way, she also used the term more generally to refer to any preconceived adverse opinion expressed about an individual, an idea, or a group of people. She was especially grieved by those whose negative views regarding others seemed unfounded or irrational, those who based their actions on ignorance even when knowledge was readily available.

The first prejudice Foote experienced was on account of racism. Some of her earliest memories were of her parents' horrifying accounts of slavery. Her father was born free but was stolen as a child and enslaved. Her mother, born a slave in New York state, was whipped mercilessly because she refused to be sexually submissive to a "very cruel master." Julia Foote personally encountered racial hostility as a young girl of ten. While working for a white family, she received a brutal lashing when the mistress falsely accused her of stealing a pound cake.

Foote recounted a number of other "indignities on account of color" as she traveled around the country in the years before the Civil War. Segregation practices, even in the North, made travel humiliating and dangerous.

In one instance, she related how she was compelled to sit outside all night on the deck of a boat—"prejudice not permitting one of my color to enter the cabin," she explained. Following that rather matter-of-fact description of the episode, Foote asked her readers a pointedly disturbing rhetorical question: "O Prejudice! thou cruel monster! wilt thou ever cease to exist?"[5]

It was in such an environment of systematic inhumanity that Foote found her humanity affirmed through redemption in Christ. When she was fifteen years old, Foote attended a Methodist quarterly meeting. As the preacher spoke on the need for repentance, Foote felt the weight of her sins on her conscience. She fell to the floor in an unconscious state and was carried home to bed. The next day, after pleading for God's mercy, she had a vision of a bright light. She "sprang from the bed . . . and commenced singing: 'Redeemed! redeemed! glory! glory!'" Julia Foote had experienced evangelical conversion; in her words, she was "saved through faith in the Lord Jesus Christ." Immediately, she took her Bible and read "the first words that caught [her] eye": "thus saith the Lord that created thee . . . fear not, for I have redeemed thee; I have called thee by thy name; thou art mine. When thou passest through the waters, I will be with thee" (Isa. 43:1–2).[6] That day, Foote received divine affirmation of her personhood, providing the encouragement she needed to stand up to the racial bias of nineteenth-century America.

In spite of the personal affirmation Foote obtained from her conversion, she was not religiously satisfied for very long. She did not feel spiritually complete, and she did not yet have the theological resources necessary to overcome all of the prejudices she had to face. Two issues bothered her particularly. First, her devotional life fluctuated wildly. Sometimes she felt close to God, at other times indifferent or full of doubt. In her words, she lived "in an up-and-down way." Secondly, Foote had a keen but unfulfilled "desire for knowledge." Although she had attended school sporadically for a few years, she now longed for more education in order that she could study her Bible, "read it with a better understanding," and write about her religious experiences. Unfortunately, circumstances were such that she did not have an opportunity for further academic instruction.

Around the year 1840, Foote tired of struggling with her "inward troubles"—namely, irresolution and a lack of knowledge. She sought a deeper experience in which she would be cleansed from sin, freed from the recurrent cycle of spiritual instability, and released from the self-deprecation that grew out of her intellectual discontent. Despite the "prejudice" of those around her who denied the possibility of anyone obtaining a "full salvation," Foote's desire for holiness was granted by God "through faith." She received sanctification, in which all known sin was cast out and "perfect love took possession" of her heart.[7]

Foote's experience of "full" salvation established a spiritual determinedness and constancy in her religious life; her faith was now "immovable." She realized that she had been "strengthened with might by [God's] Spirit in the inner man; that being rooted and grounded," she could "comprehend . . . the love of Christ which passeth knowledge." Internal spiritual strength from God provided Foote with a spiritual comprehension that far exceeded any humanly contrived knowledge. While she had only a limited education, she had been "transformed by the renewing of [her] mind" (Rom.12:1). "Though my [intellectual] gifts were but small," she confided to her readers, "I could not be shaken by what man might think or say."[8]

Foote's sanctification experience did not occur in a religious vacuum; it coincided with the historical period when evangelical Protestantism was agitated by the theological and social implications of the concept of Christian perfection. About 1840, Charles Finney started to stress sanctification in his preaching; William Goodell and other abolitionists began to interpret "holy activity" as a religious justification for the politicization of antislavery; and evangelist Phoebe Palmer (1807–1874) commenced her famous meetings for the promotion of holiness. Palmer's meetings, which attracted many influential business and ecclesiastical figures, became the nucleus of the Holiness movement, a nineteenth-century renewal of the Wesleyan concept of sanctification among Methodists and other Protestants.[9]

Until the 1870s, the Holiness movement received the blessing and endorsement of Methodist church leaders. This general attitude of acceptance changed by the 1880s, however, due to a significant transition then occurring within Methodism. During the second half of the nineteenth century, the denomination gradually assumed more and more of the trappings of middle-class culture. Many Methodists were self-consciously trying to distance themselves from the denomination's earlier image as an emotional backwoods sect. Increasingly, the exuberant preaching, ecstatic worship style, and ascetically rigorous moral demands of the Holiness evangelists were shunned by urban white Methodists and other upwardly mobile Protestants. They considered their restrained religious faith to be more sophisticated than the enthusiastic expressions of faith characteristic of African American and rural-oriented white Holiness folk, and they ridiculed Holiness preachers as "holy rollers." By the 1880s, Holiness believers felt alienated from the very churches in which they had grown up, churches that only a few decades before had practiced the same kind of preaching, worship, and morality they were advocating. Consequently, a large number of Holiness people left the major denominations by the end of the century and formed their own small splinter groups.[10] Julia Foote's spiritual odyssey spanned this entire period of Holiness history, since she received sanctification around 1840 in the beginning years of the Holiness movement, and she promoted the "second blessing" continuously until her death in 1900.

The concept of obtaining "perfect" love or "entire" sanctification may seem naively idealistic or even self-righteous today, but it is important to try to understand the doctrine from Foote's perspective. She believed that it was the privilege of every Christian believer to have an "inward, instantaneous sanctification, whereby the root . . . of sin is destroyed." In good Wesleyan fashion, she always described the experience of sanctification as an act of God's grace, not a product of human righteousness. Also, she carefully qualified her idea of perfection: "I am not teaching absolute perfection," Foote insisted, "for that belongs to God alone. Nor do I mean a state of angelic or Adamic perfection, but Christian perfection—an extinction of every temper contrary to love."[11] Thus, Foote's interpretation of holiness focused on the specific moral and ethical behavior of Christian believers toward God and one another.

Whether or not one believes in the possibility of entire sanctification, the experience was unquestionably the most important event in Julia Foote's life, and it clearly marked a turning point in her religious journey. While conversion provided affirmation of her humanity, sanctification gave her the spiritual strength to overcome any obstacle.

Foote described each of the obstacles she faced as a kind of prejudice. Collectively, all of the prejudices were the result of unspiritual, "worldly" knowledge. We have already seen how the first barrier Foote ran up against was racism. Next, she encountered many people (including her own husband) who opposed her fervent witness to the experience of holiness. She concluded that they were "prejudiced," too, by their lack of knowledge regarding true doctrine. Foote's steadfastness in facing up to hostility directed toward her race and toward her religious views stood her in good stead when she had to brave the most enduring prejudice of her life: discrimination due to her vocation as a woman evangelist.

Called to Preach

Several years after her sanctification, Foote was "impressed that God would have [her] work in his vineyard"—that is, she felt called to evangelize. Despite the fierce disapproval of her husband and her pastor, who was a well-respected African Methodist Episcopal Zion minister, Foote launched out on her own as a preacher of the gospel. When the minister came to see Foote in order to stop her flagrant disrespect for social convention, his sneering manner communicated to her that he believed she did not "know anything." In response, Foote simply replied once again that, in spite of her "very small" abilities, she could "no longer be shaken" by him or anyone else.[12] Even though the church excommunicated her, she was not daunted from her evangelistic mission. She faithfully preached the holiness message to black and white audiences throughout the northern portion of the United States, itinerating as far west as Cincinnati and as far south as Washington, D.C. Years later, in 1894, the African Methodist Episcopal Zion Church ordained Julia Foote as its first woman deacon; and, in 1900, just before her death, the denomination ordained her as its second woman elder, thereby acknowledging, albeit belatedly, her more than fifty years of preaching ministry.

Several factors helped to sustain Foote as she carried out her call to preach. First, her life situation allowed her a measure of freedom not accorded to most nineteenth-century women. She had no children, which gave her a degree of "leisure" to pursue her ministry. Also, Foote's husband worked on a ship for six months of the year, providing her with a respite from domestic duties—and from his criticism. During the years of her husband's absence, and then later following his death, Foote was supported by a "band of sisters whom [she] loved dearly." These women were her companions on preaching missions, and she "opened [her] mind" to them when she needed guidance.[13] Mutual bonds of encouragement among Christian "sisters" were often an important source of spiritual energy for women who sought to expand their vocational opportunities beyond the patriarchal church structures of nineteenth-century American Protestantism.

Foote also received encouragement for her unconventional ministry from the ethos of the Holiness movement. Many mid-nineteenth century advocates of Christian perfection, such as Finney and Goodell, were committed to enhancing the role of women in the church. They acted on these commitments even though such attitudes were in direct contrast to prevailing cultural norms. Not surprisingly, then, when various Holiness organizations broke away from mainline denominations later in the century, they were the first American churches to ordain women.

The Holiness movement offered Biblical arguments in support of women preachers. One of the best-known apologies for the scriptural basis of female ministry was presented in Phoebe Palmer's highly publicized book on the subject. Thus, when Foote sought to establish Biblical authority for her work as a preacher, she had a precedent to follow. The hermeneutical path toward a more open style of scriptural interpretation had already been pioneered by a number of Holiness women and men. Foote reflected the sentiments of these Holiness exegetes when she wrote sarcastically that St. Paul's admonition to "help those women who labor with me in the Gospel" (Phil. 4:3), "certainly meant that they did more than to pour out tea."[14]

In addition to organizational credentialing and the development of an inclusive Biblical hermeneutic, the Holiness movement contributed to the breaking down of social barriers by the application of its distinctive doctrine of entire sanctification. We have already seen how the social reform dimensions of holiness theology became evident in the lifework of William Goodell and other antislavery revivalists in the early to mid nineteenth century. While Foote's conception of sanctification built upon the revivalists' formulation of Christian perfection, some aspects of her thought diverged from their understanding. The particular form of the holiness message articulated by Julia Foote was situated in between the pre-Civil War understanding of sanctification typified by William Goodell, and the turn-of-the-twentieth-century Pentecostal understanding of sanctification typified by William Seymour.

Goodell, writing in the 1840s, expressed his holiness views in terms of certain Enlightenment categories. He surmised that truth was readily discernible to people as long as they had free access to knowledge. He also believed that individuals had the ability and the duty to act with purified volitional intent. The degree to which persons acted morally was based on the extent of their knowledge, the amount of "light" they had received. Whenever sanctified believers were introduced to new truth about God and God's will for humanity, they were required to change their behavior to be in accordance with the new understanding. In Goodell's words,

> [T]he more the Christian loves God and divine truth, and the more he walks in conformity with them, the more he will *desire* to learn, and consequently, *will* learn of them. . . . [I]t is only in the exercise of holy love . . . that the doctrines by which . . . human relations [are] revealed are . . . clearly perceived. For the holy love of God and of duty constitutes that single eye which causes the whole body to be full of light.[15]

Though Foote wrote thirty years after Goodell, she agreed with him on several points. Like Goodell, she maintained that a life of holiness resulted in a desire to learn God's will and a knowledge of "divine truth." Foote concurred with Goodell's contention that "only in the exercise of holy love" could a correct comprehension of God's standard for human relations be "clearly perceived." If "wholly sanctified" Christians "continue[d] to walk in the light," Foote wrote, then they were divinely enabled to perceive God's "understanding" regarding social and theological issues.[16]

In spite of the similarities between Goodell and Foote, changes in evangelical Protestantism during the intervening years ensured that their spiritualities would differ from each other's in some respects. Specifically, Foote put more stress on the Christian's consciousness of the supernatural; that is, she placed great importance on the Holy Spirit's direct role as the interpreter of divine truth to the believer. For Goodell, truth could be ascertained by any sincere searcher; the function of the Spirit was simply to guide Christians in their search. For Foote, truth was revealed transcendently when God poured out the Holy Spirit on men and women; the function of the Spirit was to break into human lives dramatically. "Not till the day of Pentecost," Foote declared, "did Christ's chosen ones see clearly, or have their understandings opened; and nothing short of a full baptism of the Spirit will dispel our unbelief." Only God's direct intervention could elicit a faithful apprehension of truth.[17]

Undoubtedly, aspects of Foote's belief in God's "supernatural presence"—especially her reliance on divine visions—were derived from traditional African American spirituality. But Foote's religious views also represented a general theological tendency among late nineteenth-and early twentieth-century Protestants to emphasize the work of the Holy Spirit. Note, for example, her use of the phrase "baptism of the Spirit." Anticipating Pentecostalism, Foote and other post-Civil War Holiness preachers spoke a great deal about the Spirit's immediacy—to heal physical ailments, for instance, or to mobilize Christians for service.

Although her theology prefigured the early twentieth-century emphasis on the Holy Spirit, Foote's views were also distinctly different from later formulations—thus demonstrating Foote's role as a bridge figure between antebellum revivalism and Pentecostalism. For example, while Pentecostals frequently used the terminology of "empowerment" to describe their spiritual experience, there is a relative absence of such language in Foote's theological expression. She was much more likely to write about the "light" or "illumination" received by sanctified Christians.[18]

In a few instances in her autobiography, Foote did use "power" terminology, but in these cases she always spoke about God's power—never her own.[19] This observation is important because some interpreters of nineteenth-century African American women's religious experience tend to place a great deal of stress on the "self-empowerment" of black women. Foote would have been shocked and dismayed to hear her spiritual life represented in such a way. Rather than "religious self-recovery," as one scholar has portrayed the faith of nineteenth-century black women,[20] Foote depicted her experience as a God-inspired transformation of her soul. Foote was convinced that she received her spiritual authority from a divine intervention of the Spirit, not from any kind of self-actualization.

Without a doubt, it is true that Foote and other African American women discovered an untapped internal potential through their conversion and sanctification experiences. Their entire self-identity was altered; no longer passive objects of oppression, they were now authentic actors of their own subjectivity. They were "nobodies" who had become "somebodies," to use a characteristic expression of womanist writers.[21] But did Foote "reformulate her identity" through "self-discovery," as some have claimed was typical for black women preachers?[22] Not if we take her at her word. Indeed, it seems strangely reductionistic to lift up the experiences of certain African American women without actually listening to their own descriptions of the cause of their identity change. While the personal authority that Foote received through her faith experiences did "reformulate" her identity, she was careful to explain that she did not do the reformulating herself. For Foote, it was crucial to identify the external agent of her authority— "the Lord Jesus Christ."

Worldly Prejudice versus Sanctified Wholeness

In summing up the relationship between Foote's theological ideas and her social vision, it is important to recognize her conceptualization of two types of "spirit" operating simultaneously within society: "the spirit which is in the world" (the "spirit of error") and "the Spirit which is of God" (the "Spirit of Truth" or the Holy Spirit). The worldly spirit produced a worldly kind of knowledge—referred to as "carnal reasoning." Carnal reasoning, in turn, resulted in "prejudice," a faulty judgement about others. Prejudice was the inevitable result of worldliness, which was caused by a lack of holiness. In respect to issues of race, the worldly spirit led unsanctified church members "to say to the poor and colored ones among them, 'Stand back a little.'" In respect to issues of gender related to female preaching, people who functioned according to carnal reasoning could not accurately comprehend God's Word. Among those who were unsanctified, Foote declared, even the "best men were liable to err."[23]

Foote pointed out the dissimilarity between the "spirit of error" and the "Spirit of Truth." The Spirit of Truth could "never be mistaken, nor can he inspire anything unholy." Rather, the Spirit provided clarity and enlightenment of the divine will (see John 16:13), even for unlearned persons who were deemed "foolish" by human standards. Foote related how the Holy Spirit took her—"a poor, ignorant girl"—and "help[ed her] by quickening [her] mental faculties." "[I]f we are wholly saved and live under the full sanctifying influence of the Holy Ghost," Foote opined, then "our minds will . . . be fully illuminated."[24]

Foote made a clear contrast between the opposing value systems she perceived to be operative. "We must be one or the other," Foote warned her readers. On the one hand, a lack of holiness resulted in individuals who were captivated by the spirit of the world. Without sanctification, even highly intelligent people could be prejudiced because they were governed by "carnal reasoning."[25]

On the other hand, prejudice would finally end when "all shall know the Lord, and holiness shall be written . . . upon all things in earth as well as in heaven. . . . Those who are fully in the truth cannot possess a prejudiced . . . spirit. . . . They cannot reject those whom [Christ] has received." In the experience of sanctification, Christians were baptized with the Holy Spirit, and the Spirit "impressed" people with God's truth. No matter what their level of formal education, sanctified people had full access to God's knowledge. The Spirit of Truth imparted the knowledge that "God is no respecter of persons" (Acts 10:34), an attitude of wholeness in which all of God's children were accepted as equal. In short, the opposite of prejudice due to carnal ignorance was social inclusion due to sanctified knowledge.[26]

Foote was especially concerned that Christians would fall into the spirit of error through their inordinate love for earthly things, for "worldly honor, worldly pleasure, worldly grandeur, worldly designs, and worldly pursuits are all incompatible with . . . [God's] kingdom of righteousness." Carnality was evident to Foote in such behavior as the drinking of alcohol, dancing, partygoing, and the wearing of jewelry or fancy clothing.[27] To us, Foote's list of carnal activities may seem arbitrary and moralistic; indeed, the Holiness movement was known for its legalistic moral code. Does not this preoccupation with avoiding "worldly" pursuits represent an "otherworldliness" that betrays genuine social transformation?

If we view Foote's condemnation of worldliness from the perspective of particular moral admonitions, we miss her point. First of all, the list of issues that she considered to be "worldly" included social concerns as well as personal moral habits. As we have seen, she condemned racism and sexism. She also repudiated capital punishment. And, like many Holiness people of the period, she was determined to move beyond the "sectarian spirit" of denominational pride. That is why, although she was a Methodist, she felt comfortable leading revival meetings with Daniel S. Warner (1842–1925), the founder of the Church of God.[28] The Church of God was a radical antidenominational, racially inclusive, egalitarian Holiness group that appealed to Foote's sympathies.

Beyond her mention of specific moral issues, Foote was most concerned with the general acceptance of worldliness among Christians. She worried about believers who were caught up in "the maxims and fashions of this world."[29] In this, she and other Holiness preachers rejected the middle-class enculturation taking place among most late nineteenth-century American Protestants. Holiness leaders perceived the growing consumer excesses of the society and wanted to have nothing to do with them, because to be ingrained in such materialism almost always meant a lessening of one's commitment to the poor and outcast. Perhaps it is correct, then, to describe Holiness people as "other-worldly," if by that phrase we mean that they were against many aspects of modern culture. They rejected, for instance, the premises of consumerism, individual self-interest, and middle-class acquisitiveness. By stressing the linkages between personal and social holiness, they repudiated the compartmentalization of sacred and secular spheres in modern society.

Holiness preachers encouraged American Christians to live according to the original root meaning of the word "holy." Etymologically, "holiness" and "wholeness" are both derived from the old English word "hal," meaning "healthy." Sanctification caused people to integrate their lives in a healthy, holistic way. When we view holiness as an integration of our lives toward God and neighbor—as indicated by the following selections from her autobiography—then Julia Foote's holiness message can assist us in overcoming the manifold "prejudices" of our own time.

Selections From the
Writings of Julia A. J. Foote

from A Brand Plucked From the Fire (1886)[30]

I have written this little book after many prayers to ascertain the will of God—having long had an impression to do it. I have a consciousness of obedience to the will of my dear Lord and Master.

My object has been to testify more extensively to the sufficiency of the blood of Jesus Christ to save from all sin. Many have not the means of purchasing large and expensive works on this important Bible theme.

Those who are fully in the truth cannot possess a prejudiced or sectarian spirit. As they hold fellowship with Christ, they cannot reject those whom he has received, nor receive those whom he rejects, but all are brought into a blessed harmony with God and each other.

The Christian who does not believe in salvation from all sin in this life, cannot have a constant, complete peace. The evil of the heart will rise up and give trouble. . . . But . . . "[a]sk, and ye shall receive." The blood of Jesus will not only purge your conscience from the guilt of sin, and from dead works, but it will destroy the very root of sin that is in the heart, by faith, so that you may serve the living God in the beauty of holiness.

My earnest desire is that many—especially of my own race—may be led to believe and enter into rest . . . sweet soul rest. . . .

I was converted when fifteen years old. It was on a Sunday evening at a quarterly meeting. . . . As the minister dwelt with great force and power on the . . . text, I beheld my lost condition as I never had done before. . . . No tongue can tell the agony I suffered. I fell to the floor, unconscious, and was carried home. Several remained with me all night, singing and praying. . . . In great terror I cried: "Lord, have mercy on me, a poor sinner!" . . . [A] ray of light flashed across my eyes, accompanied by a sound of far distant singing; the light grew brighter and brighter and the singing more distinct, and soon I caught the words: "This is the new song—redeemed, redeemed!" I at once sprang from the bed where I had been lying for twenty hours, without meat or drink, and commenced singing:

"Redeemed! redeemed! glory! glory!" Such joy and peace as filled my heart, when I felt that I was redeemed and could sing the new song. Thus was I wonderfully saved from eternal burning.

I hastened to take down the Bible . . . and the first words that caught my eye were: "But now, thus saith the Lord that created thee, O Jacob, and he that formed thee, O Israel, fear not, for I have redeemed thee; I have called thee by thy name; thou art mine. . . . Isaiah xliii. 1, 2

My soul cried, "Glory! glory!" and I was filled with rapture too deep for words. Was I not indeed a brand plucked from the burning? I went from house to house, telling my young friends what a dear Saviour I had found. . . .

For six months I had uninterrupted peace and joy in Jesus . . . . [Then, however,] through temptation I was brought into great distress of mind. . . . I continued to live in an up-and-down way for more than a year, when there came to our church an old man and his wife, who, when speaking in meeting, told of the trouble they once had had in trying to overcome their temper, subdue their pride, etc. But they took all to Jesus, believing his blood could wash them clean and sanctify them wholly to himself; and oh! the peace, the sweet peace, they had enjoyed ever since. Their words thrilled me through and through.

I at once understood what I needed. . . . I wanted to be sanctified. . . . [W]hile waiting on the Lord, my large desire was granted, through faith in my precious Saviour. The glory of God seemed almost to prostrate me to the floor. There was, indeed, a weight of glory resting upon me. . . . I continued day by day, month after month, to walk in the light as He is in the light, having fellowship with the Trinity. . . . The blood of Jesus Christ cleansed me from all sin. . . . And will he not do for all what he did for me? Yes, yes; God is no respecter of persons. . . .

For months I had been moved upon to exhort and pray with the people, in my visits from house to house; and in meetings my whole seemed drawn out for the salvation of souls. The love of Christ in me was not limited. Some of my mistaken friends said I was too forward, but a desire to work for the Master, and to promote the glory of his kingdom in the salvation of souls, was food to my poor soul.

When called of God, on a particular occasion, to a definite work [of preaching], I said, "No, Lord, not me." Day by day I was more impressed that God would have me work in his vineyard. I thought it could not be that I was called to preach—I, so weak and ignorant. Still, I knew all things were possible with God, even to confounding the wise by the foolish things of this earth. . . .

[M]y minister . . . came to see me. He looked very coldly upon me and said: "I guess you will find out your mistake before you are many months older." He was a scholar, and a fine speaker; and the sneering, indifferent way in which he addressed me, said most plainly: "You don't know anything." I replied: "My gifts are very small, I know, but I can no longer be shaken by what you or any one else may think or say. . . . "

Though I did not wish to pain any one, neither could I please any one only as I was led by the Holy Spirit. I saw, as never before, that the best men were liable to err, and that the only safe way was to fall on Christ, even though censure and reproach fell upon me for obeying his voice. Man's opinion weighed nothing with me, for my commission was from heaven, and my reward was with the Most High.

I could not believe that it was a short-lived impulse or spasmodic influence that impelled me to preach. I read that on the day of Pentecost was the Scripture fulfilled as found in Joel ii. 28, 29; and it certainly will not be denied that women as well as men were at that time filled with the Holy Ghost, because it is expressly stated that women were among those who continued in prayer and supplication, waiting for the fulfillment of the promise. Women and men are classed together, and if the power to preach the Gospel is short-lived and spasmodic in the case of women, it must be equally so in that of men; and if women have lost the gift of prophesy, so have men.

We are sometimes told that if a woman pretends to a Divine call, and thereon grounds the right to plead the cause of a crucified Redeemer in public, she will be believed when she shows credentials from heaven; that is, when she works a miracle. If it be necessary to prove one's right to preach the Gospel, I ask of my brethren to show me their credentials, or I can not believe in the propriety of their ministry.

But the Bible puts an end to this strife when it says: "There is neither male nor female in Christ Jesus. . . . "

Though opposed, I went forth laboring for God, and he owned and blessed my labors, and has done so wherever I have been until this day. . . .

A Word to My Christian Sisters.

DEAR SISTERS: I would that I could tell you a hundredth part of what God has revealed to me of his glory, especially on that never-to-be-forgotten night when I received my high and holy calling. The songs I heard I think were those which Job, David and Isaiah speak of hearing at night upon their beds, or the one of which the Revelator says "no man could learn." Certain it is, I have not been able to sing it since though at times I have seemed to hear the distant echo of the music. When I tried to repeat it, it vanished in the dim distance. Glory! glory! glory to the Most High!

Sisters, shall not you and I unite with the heavenly host in the grand chorus? If so, you will not let what man may say or do, keep you from doing the will of the Lord or using the gifts you have for the good of others. How much easier to bear the reproach of men than to live at distance from God. Be not kept in bondage by those who say, "We suffer not a woman to teach," thus quoting Paul's words but not rightly applying them. What though we are called to pass through deep waters, so our anchor is cast within the veil, both sure and steadfast? Blessed experience! I have had to weep because this was not my constant experience. At times, a cloud of heaviness has covered my mind, and disobedience has caused me to lose the clear witness of perfect love. . . .

Glory to God, who giveth us the victory through our Lord Jesus Christ! His blood meets all the demands of the law against us. . . .

Dear sisters in Christ, are any of you also without understanding and slow of heart to believe, as were the disciples? Although they had seen their Master do many mighty works, yet, with change of place or circumstances, they would go back upon the old ground of carnal reasoning and unbelieving fears. . . .

Not till the day of Pentecost did Christ's chosen ones see clearly, or have their understandings opened; and nothing short of a full baptism of the Spirit will dispel our unbelief. Without this, we are but babes—all our lives are often carried away by our carnal natures and kept in bondage; whereas, if we are wholly saved and live under the full sanctifying influence of the Holy Ghost, we cannot be tossed about with every wind, but, like an iron pillar or a house built upon a rock, prove immovable. Our minds will then be fully illuminated, our hearts purified, and our souls filled with the pure love of God, bringing forth fruit to his glory.

NOTES

1. The term "womanist" distinguishes the unique contribution of African American women (in fields such as literature, theology, and ethics) from the different emphases taken by European American feminist scholars. Alice Walker coined the term in her book *In Search of Our Mothers' Gardens: Womanist Prose* (New York: Harcourt Brace Jovanovich, 1983).

2. Julia A. J. Foote, *A Brand Plucked from the Fire: An Autobiographical Sketch* (Cleveland: Lauer & Yost, 1886), 3–4, 53, 116.

3. A recent reprinting of Foote's 1879 autobiography is found in William L. Andrews, ed., *Sisters of the Spirit: Three Black Women's Autobiographies of the Nineteenth Century* (Bloomington, Ind.: Indiana University Press, 1986). The references in this chapter, however, come from the 1886 printing of Foote's book.

4. Foote, 7.

5. Ibid., 96.

6. Ibid., 32–33.

7. Ibid., 43–45, 59.

8. Ibid., 116, 44, 47.

9. See Melvin Easterday Dieter, *The Holiness Revival of the Nineteenth Century* (Metuchen, N.J.: Scarecrow Press, 1980) and John L. Peters, *Christian Perfection and American Methodism* (New York: Abingdon Press, 1956).

10. Donald W. Dayton, *Discovering an Evangelical Heritage* (New York: Harper & Row, 1976).

11. Foote, 120.

12. Ibid., 65, 72.

13. Ibid., 62, 66.

14. Ibid., 79. See Phoebe Palmer, *The Promise of the Father*.

15. William Goodell, "Christian Progress," *Christian Investigator* 6 (May 1848): 500.

16. Foote, 112–15.

17. Ibid., 115.

18. Ibid., 37, 41, 43, 49, 114–16.

19. Ibid., 12, 38, 59, 92, 109.

20. Yvonne Chireau, review of Kimberly Rae Connor, *Conversions and Visions in the Writings of African-American Women,* in *Journal of the American Academy of Religion* 64 (1996): 694–95.

21. Delores S. Williams, "A Womanist Perspective on Sin," ed. Emilie Maureen Townes, *A Troubling in My Soul: Womanist Perspectives on Evil and Suffering* (Maryknoll, N.Y.: Orbis Books, 1993), 143.

22. Chireau, 694–95.

23. Foote, 11–12, 78, 116.

24. Ibid., 11, 36, 115–16.

25. Ibid., 115–17.

26. Ibid., 3, 48, 65, 96.

27. Ibid., 117–18.

28. Ibid., 3; Journal of Daniel Warner, archives of Anderson University, Anderson, Ind.

29. Foote, 117.

30. Foote, 3–4, 32–34, 36, 40, 43, 47–48, 65, 71–72, 78–79, 80, 112–13, 114, 115–116.

3.

WILLIAM SEYMOUR
(1870–1922)

Pentecostal Leader of the Azusa Street Revival:
Empowered to Bring All Races
Into One Common Family

The scandals involving televangelists Jim Bakker and Jimmy Swaggert reinforced in the public mind many longstanding negative perceptions about Pentecostals. Indeed, from the very beginning of the Pentecostal movement—and especially since the 1925 publication of *Elmer Gantry*, Sinclair Lewis's devastating caricature of a flamboyant, self-promoting minister—charismatic preachers have been stereotyped by disparaging characterizations. A typical description portrays Pentecostals as blind followers of doomsday evangelists who advocate ecstatic worship and a rigid (but hypocritically unobserved) code of moral behavior. Many mainline Protestants view Pentecostalism critically because they believe that the movement has fostered a self-absorbed individualism—stressing personal experience and spectacular religious phenomena to the neglect of justice issues. Such critics may also assume that Pentecostals spend their time speculating about the end times instead of solving the more urgent social problems of today.

Those who have held an unfavorable impression of the social conscience of charismatic Christians might be surprised to learn about William Seymour, an African American preacher who was one of the leading figures of early Pentecostalism. Seymour's understanding of the power of the Holy Spirit included an emphasis on glossolalia, the speaking in unknown tongues. But Seymour's religious faith went much deeper than just the practice of charismatic gifts, for it was based on an eschatological vision of God's desire for interracial harmony. Consequently, this self-effacing evangelist devoted himself to preaching a spirituality of empowerment intended to lead the church toward a radical transformation of individuals and society.

Seymour in Context

Seymour grew up in the post-Civil War period, when Protestant Christianity, along with other social institutions in the United States, was undergoing growth pains associated with the increasing industrialization of the United States. The expanding economic might of the nation was based on the rise of global markets as the United States became a world power. As Americans learned more about the outside world, they became less parochial. Unfortunately, many Americans also became more domineering, adopting the Eurocentric idea that Westerners had a "white man's burden" to bring "civilization" and Christianity to the world. In the church, these imperialistic pretensions coincided with an increased interest in foreign missions.

Vast improvements in transportation technology encouraged the cosmopolitan mind-set. The development of a national network of railroads, for instance, helped to create a more mobile population. Christians heralded the improved transportation as a way to spread the gospel message. In the minds of many religious people, the United States appeared to be poised for unprecedented advancement, both spiritually and economically. Among those Christians who profited from the business expansion of the era, the nation's overall condition seemed extremely positive. Protestant churches were growing in membership, contributions were increasing, and thousands of opulent neo-Gothic church structures were being built. Adding to this confident interpretation of the nation's situation was the popularity of a theory known as social Darwinism, which hypothesized that human society—and especially U.S. society—was advancing according to immutable laws of evolutionary progress. Many leading Christian thinkers in the late nineteenth century accepted these "progressive" ideas and reshaped them to fit into a religious mold. The result was an ebullient belief that God had placed a special blessing on America's endeavors for social improvement.[1]

Not all Americans interpreted the national scene with the same sanguine expectations as those who benefitted from the nation's economic growth. The industrial expansion was not without its difficulties, for it inevitably caused periodic financial panics. Those on the margins of society were especially vulnerable to fiscal fluctuations. The underprivileged did not view social opportunity with the exuberance that characterized the attitudes of the upwardly mobile people who capitalized on the economic boom.

The socioeconomic situation was particularly grim for African Americans. The newly freed Southern slaves wanted to escape from the virulent racism of the region and their endemically lower-class status. Many of them availed themselves of the new accessibility to transportation and traveled by train to Northern and Western urban centers such as Chicago, Cincinnati,

Detroit, and Los Angeles. Unfortunately, what greeted them in those cities was not necessarily an improvement in their social or economic condition. Even on their train trip to northern "opportunity," African Americans were humiliated by segregated seating. Typically, a curtain divided the forward section of the train reserved for whites from the section in the back designated for "colored" people. Segregation of public accommodations was given official sanction by the infamous 1896 Supreme Court decision upholding "separate but equal" interstate train service.

Those Americans who found themselves in a place of social and financial struggle—whether blacks or the dispossessed of any race—could not identify with the optimism held by religious Progressives. They could not imagine that the Kingdom of God would evolve here on earth, as many socially affluent Christians envisioned. While hopeful of their future place in heaven, poor men and women placed little hope in their present existence. They were not convinced that the temporal order could be improved incrementally by human efforts; only God's sudden intervention could change this sinful world. Such people were drawn toward premillennialism, an eschatological doctrine that became popular among many evangelical Protestants in the decades following the Civil War.

The prevalence of premillennialism in the post-War period was evident in the number of Holiness preachers who switched from postmillennialism to premillennialism. According to the theological perspective of Charles Finney, William Goodell, and their postmillennial colleagues in the optimistic years before the Civil War, the thousand-year reign of God on earth would be established gradually when Christians followed God's sanctified will for humanity. But according to the premillennialists who came into prominence in the period of social flux after the War, Christ would break into human history dramatically to set up his Kingdom. Wars, "rumors of wars," famines, pestilences, and earthquakes were all signs of Christ's impending judgment. Just prior to this imminent "second coming" of Christ, believers would be miraculously swept away from the wickedness of the present world and "raptured" into God's presence.

Many premillennialists believed that God's plan for humanity was expressed differently in successive historical eras. The final era was to be the age of the Holy Spirit, associated with the coming millennial Kingdom. Holiness-oriented premillennialists at the end of the nineteenth century put special emphasis on the immediacy of the Spirit. They were convinced that signs of the Spirit's millennial outpouring were beginning to be experienced by sanctified believers. They felt that they had entered the period of the "latter rain" of God's blessings as foretold by the prophet Joel (2:23–29). Julia Foote's linkage of the experience of sanctification with the "baptism of the Spirit" was indicative of this increased interest in the immediacy of religious experience.

Holiness preachers were not shy about their thoughts as to what spiritual conditions were necessary to bring about the promised second coming. The paramount condition was the conversion and sanctification of souls—"getting right with God." The church must become holy before the rapture can take place. But how, they asked, would the church's holiness be evident? Increasingly, their understanding of Christian holiness came to include a manifestation of sensational signs of the Spirit such as physical healing and ecstatic worship.

By the turn of the twentieth century, some Holiness leaders began to interpret the Biblical text of the first Pentecost (Acts 2) as paradigmatic for the spirituality of contemporary Christians. These preachers came to be known as "Pentecostals," and when they read the Scriptures, they found several specific characteristics of the Spirit's manifestation: glossolalia, the power to witness Christ to the nations, and the unity of all believers. Many Pentecostals understood the last point as a call for Christians to break down social distinctions of denomination, class, gender, and race. This Pentecostal emphasis on the spiritual unity of Christians fit well with the anti-elitist positions of the Holiness movement, which had rejected the middle-class values of mainline Protestant social respectability. The Pentecostals' doctrine of tongues, however, was much more controversial, and the differences of opinion regarding the validity of glossolalia instigated a bitter division within the Holiness movement, a division that had an important effect on the ministry of William Seymour.

Seymour and the
"Azusa Miracle"

Seymour was born during the Reconstruction era in Centerville, Louisiana.[2] Little is known of his early years, except that he actively participated in the African American church in his community. Most Southern blacks like Seymour practiced a type of Christianity that amalgamated Protestant evangelicalism with aspects of their African religious heritage: spiritual practices were communally oriented; worship focused on rhythm, spontaneity, and evocative preaching; the indwelling of the Spirit was experienced through a Christ-centered conversion; and symbolic imagery, derived from the Bible, became the foundation of their spirituality. Seymour thus inherited a vital, indigenized Christian faith.[3]

When he was twenty-five years old, Seymour took the route travelled by many freedmen; he went North in search of better employment. In Seymour's case, he journeyed to Indianapolis, and found work as a waiter in a downtown hotel. He joined the waiter's union and the local black Methodist Episcopal Church.

Not long afterward, Seymour moved to Cincinnati, where he became affiliated with the Holiness movement. He joined the fellowship of the "Evening Light Saints," an interracial evangelistic organization that ordained him to preach. The Evening Light Saints later became a part of the Church of God, the same egalitarian Holiness group with which Julia Foote preached toward the end of her life. As noted in the last chapter, the Church of God was known for its antidenominational stance and its broadmindedness on issues of racial and gender equality. Therefore, during his stay in Ohio, Seymour acquired a strong commitment to radical Holiness ideas such as the immediacy of the Spirit and the inclusiveness of the Church.

In 1903, Seymour returned to the South in search of long-lost relatives. After locating family members in Texas, he settled there for a while, using Houston as a base for his evangelistic forays to other cities. He also became acquainted with Charles F. Parham (1873–1929), a white Pentecostal preacher and Bible college instructor who was visiting Houston. Parham had gained notoriety in 1901 when he and some of his Bible college students claimed to be the first modern-day Christians to speak in tongues. Though Parham had been a Holiness evangelist, his doctrinal teaching in support of the practice of glossolalia deviated from standard Holiness beliefs. Typically, Holiness preachers taught that the baptism with the Holy Spirit was simultaneous with the experience of sanctification, not with the gift of tongues.

In 1905, Seymour attended a series of Bible lectures delivered by Parham on the subject of Spirit baptism. Although Seymour had not yet experienced the gift of tongues for himself, he accepted Parham's doctrinal justification of the practice. Seymour developed a theological affinity for Parham's views in spite of the fact that Parham was a racist. Parham refused to allow Seymour to congregate with the white students in the class. In order that he could listen to the Bible lesson, Seymour had to sit in the next room with the door ajar. Even at revival meetings, Parham did not permit blacks to pray at the altar together with whites.

While the Holiness movement was relatively unprejudiced in comparison to the extreme amount of racism that prevailed generally within organized religion, Parham's segregationist practice indicates that the pervasive racial bigotry of the period had an impact upon every religious group. The decades leading up to and just after the turn of the twentieth century have been referred to as the nadir of race relations in the United States. Jim Crow laws kept African Americans legally segregated, and more informal kinds of discrimination were maintained at every level of society. Especially gruesome was the rising influence of the Ku Klux Klan and the alarming increase in lynching incidents, reaching an average of thirteen per month in the years from 1884 to 1900.[4]

In the midst of this climate of racial prejudice—some of which Seymour had experienced firsthand—Seymour accepted an invitation in 1906 to become the pastor of a fledgling Holiness congregation in Los Angeles. During the early years of the twentieth century, Los Angeles was a booming small city with an amazing diversity of ethnic communities: Anglo, African American, Mexican, Chinese, and others. There was a degree of openness to new people and new ideas in southern California not found elsewhere. California's receptivity to religious innovation was similar in some ways to the role played by the "burned-over district" of New York state during the early nineteenth century, when Finney and Goodell crusaded for revivalistic social reform.[5]

When Seymour began to preach his recently learned doctrine of tongues as the initial evidence of the baptism with the Holy Spirit, the Holiness folks who had invited him to come to Los Angeles forbade him to pastor their congregation any longer. Undaunted, Seymour shared his Pentecostal message with a home fellowship group. Soon, large crowds started to go to the house meetings, and some people began to speak in tongues. A defining moment occurred in April 1906, when Seymour received the gift of tongues for himself. Scores of other men and women followed his example.

With so many people going to the services, the meetings began to receive attention from the daily newspapers. Reporters attended the services and then wrote derisive accounts of the charismatic gifts that were displayed. They often ridiculed Seymour as a "self-appointed negro prophet." One correspondent for the *Los Angeles Times* wrote mockingly about a worshipper who "prophesied awful destruction to this city unless its citizens are brought to a belief in the tenets of the new faith." The reporter's article had unintended consequences, for it was featured in the paper on the same day that another more famous story captured the headlines: the San Francisco earthquake.[6] Given the uncanny connection between these seemingly apocalyptic events, more and more people started attending Seymour's Pentecostal meetings.

Seymour and his associates recognized the need for additional space, but they had very little money for a church. They purchased an inexpensive building on Azusa Street, in a poor section of the city, and designated it as the Apostolic Faith Mission. The structure had formerly been an African Methodist Episcopal church; more recently it had been used as a warehouse and a stable. The tumbledown building became the center for religious exercises that ran nearly nonstop for three and a half years. This continuous series of evangelistic worship services is referred to collectively as the "Azusa Street Revival."

The humble origins of worldwide Pentecostalism at Azusa Street took on mythic proportions; among charismatics, the lowly location is frequently compared to another stable birthplace that occurred nineteen hundred years earlier. While scholars may not be willing to grant Azusa Street the lofty symbolic status that Pentecostals accord to it, most will agree that this location served an important function for early Pentecostalism. The plain meetinghouse created a physical and spiritual space for people to worship interracially in an era when integrated religious fellowship was not allowed within standard, more formalized church settings.

Indeed, one of the most significant aspects of the Azusa Street meetings was their inclusiveness. From the beginning of the revival, blacks and whites attended the services in nearly equal numbers. Occasionally there were also Mexican Americans, Chinese Americans, Native Americans, and people from other ethnic backgrounds. Newspapers wrote disparagingly of this clear break with social custom, while participants spoke of the mixed-race meetings as the "Azusa miracle."

The Whole Gospel: The Apostolic Faith for "One Common Family"

Without taking away from the supernatural element present at Azusa Street, it is important to realize that the specific content of William Seymour's spirituality—what he called "the whole gospel"—led directly to the integrative aspects of the revival. "Nothing less than the whole Gospel of Jesus Christ," Seymour proclaimed, "will suffice in these last days." Sometimes Pentecostals still refer to their spiritual message as the "full gospel," but they usually use the phrase to point solely to the modern recovery of the charismatic gifts. For Seymour, the fullness of the gospel meant a complete restoration of the apostolic faith of the early church. In his view, the love and unity of Christians was the primary mark of apostolic faith, while the gift of tongues was merely an evidence of that unity.[7]

Pivotal to Seymour's theology was his premillennial belief in the imminent earthly return of Jesus. As with many evangelicals at the turn of the twentieth century, Seymour was convinced that Christ would come soon "as a thief in the night" (1 Thess. 5:2) to take his people to be with him before the great judgment day. After the rapture took place, believers would "help Him rule this old world in the millemnium [sic], when righteousness shall cover the earth."[8] Seymour's eschatological views were no different from those of other premillennialists of the period. In fact, his ideas about the end times, his literal interpretation of the Bible, and his acceptance of most traditional doctrines placed Seymour's theology in agreement with the beliefs of other fundamentalist premillennialists of the period.

However, adherence to premillennialism did not result in a world-denying attitude for Seymour, as it did for some conservative Christians who stressed the literal, imminent return of Christ. There were two sources for Seymour's stress on this-worldly concerns: his African American religious heritage and his theological emphasis on sanctification and the baptism with the Holy Spirit.

The role that Christianity played in the struggle for racial justice has been hotly debated by African American historians. Some scholars, such as E. Franklin Frazier, state that blacks' wide-scale acceptance of Christianity resulted in an attitude of lethargic docility in the face of injustice.[9] Other historians, such as Vincent Harding, believe that the effect of Christianity on the social conscience of black Americans was more varied than that described by Frazier. According to Harding, the African American gospel had a double message—one that encouraged survivalistic accommodation to oppression on the one hand and bold resistance to oppression on the other.[10]

Several scholars have recognized that African Americans developed an inherent religious concern for social justice. This social concern was due to two factors. First, black Americans drew much of their religious worldview from the traditional African concept that all of life is an organic whole. Second, they lived under the constant burden of racism; the fear of violence and the relentlessness of economic deprivation created a situation in which the articulation of social needs was literally a matter of life and death.[11]

These factors were not present among Christians of European descent, and the majority of nineteenth- and twentieth-century whites accepted the prevailing cultural split between sacred and secular realms, between piety and social witness. Most black Christians, at least before the 1920s, could not fathom such a division. African American spirituality encouraged both an intense personal piety and a commitment to social justice. Sheer socioeconomic destitution compelled African Americans to make social issues central in their churches, while the ecstatic expression of devotion to God was an established practice of corporate black worship. Seymour drew from this African American legacy of holistic spirituality.[12]

Along with the social ethic derived from his ethnic religious heritage, Seymour also inherited a tradition of social involvement when he became part of the Holiness movement. As we have seen in the life stories of William Goodell and Julia Foote, the nineteenth-century religious concentration on the experience of sanctification was a forceful impulse toward social transformation. Seymour supplemented this Holiness concept of sanctification with the Pentecostal emphasis on the empowerment of the Spirit, thereby altering somewhat the nineteenth-century rendering of sanctification.[13]

When Seymour articulated his theology in a systematic fashion, he began in typical Protestant form with an affirmation of the doctrine of justification, which he linked to the experience of conversion. Next, he stated his belief in sanctification, the "second . . . work of grace," which cleansed Christians of inbred sin. The third step of the Christian life for Seymour was the baptism with the Holy Spirit. Unlike Julia Foote and other Holiness preachers, who equated the experience of sanctification with the baptism with the Holy Spirit, Seymour separated these spiritual events. According to his understanding, God gave Spirit baptism as an additional experience to any sanctified believer who prayed for it—"a gift of power upon the sanctified life." In summary, Seymour taught that God's plan of salvation included "two works of grace [justification and sanctification] and the gift of the Holy Spirit."[14]

Seymour believed that Spirit baptism was the religious objective to which all Christians should aspire—"the privilege of everyone." The baptism with the Holy Ghost was each believer's "personal Pentecost," supplying men and women with a special endowment of God's power. Indeed, the availability of divine empowerment was the most essential attribute in Seymour's theology. "Holy Ghost power" offered emotional, physical, and spiritual healing from personal problems such as addiction, depression, bodily ailments, and suicidal thoughts. It also provided Christians with the ability to evangelize effectively. Along with many other American Christians during this time, Seymour was preoccupied with sharing the gospel—to his immediate neighbors and even "to the uttermost parts of the earth" (Acts 1:8).[15]

This is the point at which the practice of glossolalia fit into Seymour's theology. Speaking in tongues, he wrote, functioned "like a bell, ringing the people up" from spiritual slumber—enlivening the faith of believers and witnessing the power of God to unbelievers. As in the apostolic period, God now provided miraculous signs for the edification of the church and the conversion of the world. "The gift of languages is given with the commission, 'Go ye into all the world and preach the Gospel.'"[16] Seymour's conviction that glossolalia stimulated effective missionary evangelism inspired him to promote the practice with great fervency.

Nonetheless, tongues-speaking was not the centerpiece of his theology, as it would be for many later Pentecostals. Glossolalia was not to be viewed as the goal of the Christian life; rather, Seymour believed, it was a spiritual bonus given to Christians. "Tongues are . . . a gift that God throws in with the baptism with the Holy Spirit"—a divine dividend. Seymour did not require speaking in tongues as the standard for religious fellowship. Instead of insisting that Christians practice glossolalia immediately, he recognized that the gift would come to sanctified believers "sooner or later"—in God's time.[17]

Seymour stated specifically that spiritual "gifts cannot save us." In fact, he asserted that "many people are going to hell trusting in gifts." Such people relied on the ecstasy of religious experience while ignoring God's primary expectation for faithful living: that Christians be in right relationship with one another. "The Word tells us that without love we are nothing."

Charity, Seymour taught, manifested the "real evidence of the baptism in every day life." The fruit of the Spirit superceded the gifts of the Spirit.[18]

According to Seymour, the most important characteristic of the baptism with the Holy Spirit was the creation of a new spiritual community in which Christians of different races and backgrounds were "in one accord." Paradoxically, unity in Christ presupposed the acceptance of differentiation in culture. Seymour was convinced that this principle—Christian commonality based on mutual respect—was "Jesus' standard" for the baptism with the Holy Spirit. It was also the "Azusa standard," as demonstrated at the revival meetings.

Seymour knew that the expression of love for such varied types of people could only come about as an outgrowth of God-given humility: "The baptism of the Holy Spirit makes you more humble and filled with divine love." Instead of "glorying" in one's own ethnicity, accomplishments, or material prosperity, Seymour encouraged each person to treat others equally, as God does: "recogniz[ing] no flesh, no color, no names." In the midst of racial, religious, and economic tensions, Seymour counseled his fellow Pentecostals to "honor every bit of God there is in one another"—certainly a relevant admonition for us, who have to deal with the "culture wars" of our own era.[19]

Seymour frequently used the image of a family to describe the Christian mutuality he envisioned for the Church. The Apostolic Mission at Azusa Street operated as "one spiritual family," in which personal differences remained but a commonality in Christ linked people together. At the revival meetings, "all classes and nationalities [met] on a common level." "No instrument that God can use," Seymour preached, "is rejected on account of color or dress or lack of education." White, black, brown, and red Pentecostals, according to a Native American preacher, were all part of one "big Holy Ghost tribe."[20]

The congregants at Azusa transcended the social distinctions commonly adhered to by the broader culture. They denied the divisiveness of denominations. They washed each other's feet in the manner of the early church (and in the manner of the Church of God, from whom Seymour first learned about integrated worship). Blacks held positions of spiritual leadership over whites. Women preached to men. Children exhorted their elders. Mexican Americans testified to English-speakers in their own Spanish language—and in unknown languages.

Seymour believed wholeheartedly that "God [wa]s drawing His people together and making them one." In preparation for Christ's second coming, God was "melting all races and nations together." By his death, Jesus had "broken down the middle wall of partition" (Eph. 2:14) between various estranged groups—in effect, tearing down the curtain that figuratively (and literally, on the trains) had divided blacks and whites. Seymour's gospel was simple: Jesus wanted to bring "all races and nations into one common family." This was a message that, he was convinced, many people had "been longing for for years." Consequently, Pentecostalism spread all over the globe from Azusa Street.[21]

The vision of interracial unity also created intense opposition, for it challenged the prevailing segregationist social order. Mixed-race Pentecostal meetings were attacked by white mobs. The dominant white religious culture regularly belittled Pentecostalism because of its "lowly black origins." Even within Pentecostalism, some of the white leaders of the movement denounced the integrated character of the Azusa revival.[22]

In the fall of 1908, one of Seymour's coworkers at Azusa Street absconded with the address list for his weekly newspaper, *The Apostolic Faith*. This prevented Seymour from reaching people outside of Los Angeles with his message. Meanwhile, doctrinal and racial divisions splintered the nascent Pentecostal movement. Pentecostal churches began to emphasize Spirit baptism as a routinized experience and disregarded Seymour's stress on the necessity of integrated fellowship. Many African American congregations, especially after World War I, retreated into privatistic piety and moralism, neglecting their earlier commitment to social change. Feeling disillusioned and betrayed, Seymour died "of a broken heart" in 1922.[23]

Despite Seymour's personal disappointment, the Azusa Street revival provides a model of a multicultural Christian community transformed by the power of the Holy Spirit. And the impact of Seymour's words still resounds over these many decades.

Selections From the Writings of William Seymour

from *The Apostolic Faith* (1906–1908)[24]

We preach old-time repentance, old-time conversion, old-time sanctification, and old-time baptism with the Holy Ghost, which is the gift of power upon the sanctified life, and God throws in the gift of tongues.

1st. Justification deals with our actual sins. When we go to Him and repent, God washes all the guilt and pollution out of our hearts, and we stand justified like a new babe that never committed sin. We have no condemnation. We can walk with Jesus and live a holy life before the Lord, if we walk in the Spirit.

2nd. Sanctification is the second and last work of grace. After we are justified, we have two battles to fight. There is sin inside and sin outside. There is warfare within, caused by the old inherited sin. When God brings the word, "It is the will of God, even your sanctification," we should accept the word, and then the blood comes and takes away all inherited sin.

Everything is heavenly in your soul, you are a son of God. The Spirit of God witnesses in your heart that you are sanctified.

3rd. The Spirit begins then and there leading us on to the Baptism with the Holy Ghost. Now, as a son of God, you should enter into the earnest [pledge] of your inheritance. After you have a clear witness of the two works of grace in your heart, you can receive this gift of God, which is a free gift without repentance. Pray for the power of the Holy Ghost, and God will give you a new language. It is the privilege of everyone to be filled with the Holy Ghost. It is for every believing child. . . .

There is a great difference between a sanctified person and one that is baptized with the Holy Ghost and fire. A sanctified person is cleansed and filled with divine love, but the one that is baptized with the Holy Ghost has the power of God on his soul and has power with God and men. . . .

Nothing less than the whole Gospel of Jesus Christ will suffice in these last days. . . .

Christ is coming again, not as the babe of Bethlehem, to be spit upon and mocked but He is coming in power and great glory. . . .

There will be two appearances of Jesus under one coming. The first appearance is called the Rapture, when He comes as a thief in the night and catches away His bride; the second is called the Revelation when He shall come with ten thousand of His saints and destroy the wicked with the brightness of His coming, and when His feet shall touch the same mount from which He ascended. But we want to be ready for the first appearance, to be caught up. We must be caught up with Him, before we can come back with Him.

Nothing but holy people will meet the Lord Jesus in the skies, when He comes in the rapture. Those that had no light on the baptism with the Holy Ghost but were sanctified will have part in the first resurrection. . . . So we see the first resurrection is of the holy people. . . .

Jesus is coming to be King over all the earth and reign from sea to sea. . . . We are going to help Him rule this old world in the millemnium [sic], when righteousness shall cover the earth as waters cover the sea. Then afterwards at the white throne judgement, we shall sit with Him and judge the world. Then after the new heavens and new earth, when He shall have delivered up the kingdom into the Father's hands, we shall reign with Him throughout eternity. O beloved, are you ready?

Jesus said, "Sell that thou hast and give to the poor". . . . Where do we find people that are doing that? . . . The Bible tells of a time when men and women will be living at ease in Zion. They will be buying houses and lands and taking their ease; but, lo, suddenly there comes a little shout in the air. The saints have been taken away; the great tribulation is on the world. They will wonder what has happened. . . . Some may laugh now in the face of God, but O when that day comes, the rich man will howl and call for the rocks to fall upon him. They will try to find some little saint of God to have them offer up a little prayer. But it will be too late. . . .

The question has been asked, How do we know as to the soon coming of the Lord, and what are the signs of His coming? . . . O may God help us to see that we are living in the fulfillment of the signs of the time. . . . [One] proof we find in the times of refreshing we are now having from the presence of the Lord. . . . We thank God for the refreshing times, the times of restitution, when God is restoring the church back to light and power and glory, and she is becoming a burning and shining light to this world again. . . .

The early rain that God sent was on the day of Pentecost, in the early morning of the apostolic age, which is the outpouring of the Spirit. And in these last days, He is sending the refreshing times, the latter rain, another Pentecost. Bless His holy name! . . .

One token of the Lord's coming is that He is melting all races and nations together, and they are filled with the power and glory of God. He is baptizing by one spirit into one body and making up a people that will be ready to meet Him when He comes. . . .

Jesus gave the church at Pentecost the great lesson of how to carry on a revival, and it would be well for every church to follow Jesus' standard of the baptism of the Holy Ghost and fire.

"And when the day of Pentecost was fully come, they were all with one accord in one place." O beloved, there is where the secret is: **one accord, one place, one heart, one soul, one mind, one prayer.** If God can get a people anywhere in one accord and in one place, of one heart, mind, and soul, believing for this great power, it will fall and Pentecostal results will follow. Glory to God!

Apostolic Faith doctrine means one accord, one soul, one heart. May God help every child of His to live in Jesus' prayer: "That they all may be one, as Thou, Father, art in Me and I in Thee; that they all may be one in us; that the world may believe that Thou hast sent Me." Praise God! O how my heart cries out to God in these days that He would make every child of His see the necessity of living in the 17th chapter of John, that we may be one in the body of Christ, as Jesus has prayed. . . .

The Lord did great things in 1906. Pentecost first fell in Los Angeles on

April 9th. Since then the good tidings has [sic] spread in two hemispheres. Many are rejoicing in pardon, purity, and the power of the Holy Ghost. Wherever the work goes, souls are saved, and not only saved from hell but through and through, and prepared to meet the Lord at His coming. Hundreds have been baptized with the Holy Ghost. . . .

It is a continual upper room tarrying at Azusa Street. It is like a continual camp-meeting or convention. All classes and nationalities meet on a common level. One who came for the first time said, "The thing that impressed me most was the humility of the people, and I went to my room and got down on my knees and asked God to give me humility . . . "

We must give God all the glory in this work. We must keep very humble at His feet. He recognizes no flesh, no color, no names. We must not glory in Azusa Mission, nor in anything but the Lord Jesus Christ by whom the world is crucified unto us and we unto the world.

We stand as assemblies and missions all in perfect harmony. Azusa Mission stands for the unity of God's people everywhere. God is uniting His people, baptizing them by one Spirit into one body. . . .

The work began among the colored people. God baptized several sanctified wash women with the Holy Ghost, who have been much used of Him. The first white woman to receive the Pentecost and gift of tongues in Los Angeles was Mrs. Evans. . . . Since then multitudes have come. God makes no difference in nationality, Ethiopians, Chinese, Indians, Mexicans, and other nationalities worship together.

No instrument that God can use is rejected on account of color or dress or lack of education. This is why God has so built up the work. . . .

It is the privilege of all the members of the bride of Christ to prophesy, which means testify or preach. . . . [W]hen our Lord poured out Pentecost, He brought all those faithful women with the other disciples into the upper room, and God baptized them all in the same room and made no difference. All the women received the anointed oil of the Holy Ghost and were able to preach the same as the men. . . . It is the same Holy Spirit in the woman as in the man. . . .

It is the Blood of Jesus that brings fellowship among the Christian family. The Blood of Jesus Christ is the strongest in the world. It makes all races and nations into one common family in the Lord and makes them all satisfied to be one. The Holy Ghost is the leader and He makes all one as Jesus prayed, "that they all may be one."

The Pentecostal power, when you sum it all up, is just more of God's love. If it does not bring more love, it is simply a counterfeit. Pentecost means to live right in the 13th chapter of First Corinthians, which is the standard. When you live there, you have no trouble to keep salvation. This is Bible religion. It is not manufactured religion. Pentecost makes us love Jesus more and love our brothers more. It brings us all into one common family.

NOTES

1. Richard Hofstadter, *Social Darwinism in American Thought, 1860–1915* (Philadelphia: University of Pennsylvania Press, 1945).

2. The only scholarly biography of Seymour is a doctoral thesis, Douglas J. Nelson, "For Such a Time As This: The Story of Bishop William J. Seymour and the Azusa Street Revival" (Ph.D. diss., University of Birmingham, England, 1981).

3. Albert J. Raboteau, *Slave Religion: The "Invisible Institution" in the Antebellum South* (Oxford: Oxford University Press, 1978), 148–49; Jamie Phelps, "Black Spirituality," in Robin Maas and Gabriel O'Donnell, *Spiritual Traditions for the Contemporary Church* (Nashville: Abingdon Press, 1990), 334–45; William E. Montgomery, *Under Their Own Vine and Fig Tree: The African-American Church in the South, 1865–1900* (Baton Rouge, La.: Louisiana State University Press, 1993), 349.

4. Nelson, 32, 40; Gayraud S. Wilmore, *Black Religion and Black Radicalism* (Garden City, N.Y.: Doubleday & Co., 1972), 190–94.

5. Sandra Sizer Frankiel, *California's Spiritual Frontiers: Religious Alternatives in Anglo-Protestantism, 1850–1910* (Berkeley, Ca.: University of California Press, 1988).

6. *Los Angeles Daily Times* (18 April 1906), cited in Nelson, 195.

7. *The Apostolic Faith* 1, no. 2 (October 1906): 4; 2, no. 13 (May 1908): 3.

8. *The Apostolic Faith* 1, no. 10 (September 1907): 4.

9. E. Franklin Frazier, *The Negro Church in America* (Liverpool: University of Liverpool, 1963).

10. Vincent Harding, "Religion and Resistance Among Antebellum Negroes, 1800–1860," in August Meier and Elliott Rudwick, eds., *The Making of Black America* (New York: Antheneum Publishers, 1969), 179–97; Raboteau, 308, 314–18.

11. Phelps, 332–40; Wilmore, 2–5.

12. Iain MacRobert, *The Black Roots and White Racism of Early Pentecostalism in the USA* (New York: St. Martin's Press, 1988), 5–36.

13. Ibid., 37–42; Donald W. Dayton, *The Theological Roots of Pentecostalism* (Peabody, Mass.: Hendrickson, 1990).

14. *The Apostolic Faith* 1, no. 1 (September 1906): 2, 3.

15. *The Apostolic Faith* 1, no. 1 (September 1906): 3; 1, no. 3 (November 1906): 1; 1, no. 6 (February–March 1907): 7.

16. *The Apostolic Faith* 1, no. 1 (September 1906): 1; 1, no. 2 (October 1906): 4.

17. *The Apostolic Faith* 1, no. 11 (January 1908): 2.

18. *The Apostolic Faith* 2, no. 13 (May 1908): 2; (June–September 1907): 2.

19. *The Apostolic Faith* 1, no. 5 (January 1907): 1; 2, no. 13 (May 1908): 2; 1, no. 2 (October 1906): 4.

20. *The Apostolic Faith* 1, no. 6 (February–March 1907): 7; 1, no. 5 (January 1907): 1, 3; 1, no. 7 (September 1907): 2; 1, no. 3 (September 1906): 1, 3; 1, no. 12 (January 1908): 2; 1, no. 3 (November 1906): 1, 4; 1, no. 2 (October 1906): 4.

21. *The Apostolic Faith* 1, no. 2 (October 1906): 4; 1, no. 7 (April 1907): 3.

22. Grant Wacker, "Travail of a Broken Family: Evangelical Responses to Pentecostalism in America, 1906–1916," *Journal of Ecclesiastical History* 47, no. 3 (July 1996): 513n; Walter J. Hollenweger, "Pentecostals and the Charismatic Movement," in Cheslyn Jones et al., eds., *The Study of Spirituality* (New York: Oxford University Press, 1986), 550–51.

23. Wilmore, 221; Phelps, 341; MacRobert, 60–76.

24. *The Apostolic Faith* 1, no. 1 (September 1906): 3; 2, no. 13 (May 1908): 3; 1, no. 2 (October 1906): 4; 1, no. 10 (September 1907): 4; 1, no. 6 (February–March 1907): 6, 7; 1, no. 5 (January 1907): 1; 1, no. 3 (November 1906): 1; 1, no. 12 (January 1908): 2; 1, no. 7 (April 1907): 3.

4.

CHARLES STELZLE
(1869–1941)

The Presbyterian "Apostle to Labor":
Promoting a Social Service Revival

C harles Stelzle challenged the conventional twentieth-century split between personal conversion and public action. When Stelzle's biography is surveyed in light of the dualistic categories usually used to describe American Christianity, it appears as if his life were filled with self-contradiction. On the one hand, Stelzle's career epitomized religious progressivism and a commitment to the social gospel. He was a union member, a defender of organized labor, a featured speaker at American Federation of Labor (A.F.of L.) conventions, a Progressive Party candidate for state office, and the founder and chief executive officer of the first Protestant social service agency. On the other hand, Stelzle faithfully represented a traditional evangelical perspective. He was an alumnus of Moody Bible Institute, a self-described theological conservative, a dedicated Prohibitionist, and a lifelong evangelist. In truth, Stelzle combined these diverse commitments into a unified vision of "social service revivalism," which he promoted by his activities on behalf of both individual and structural salvation. He hoped to end the needless antagonism separating evangelists and social activists.[1]

While Stelzle saw no contradiction in his multifaceted convictions, many of his contemporaries did. Extremists on either side of the religious divide were not comfortable with the way in which he successfully bridged the tensions between evangelism and the social gospel. His predicament was made especially difficult because he served as a minister in the northern Presbyterian Church—the denomination most affected by the fundamentalist/modernist controversy—during the years in which the worst theological divisiveness prevailed. Consequently, more than any other person in this book, Charles Stelzle had to contend with the fierce polarization of the two-party system in American Protestantism. To his credit, his steadfastness in preaching "a larger, fuller gospel" helped to demonstrate the cogency of an integrated, multidimensional religious faith.[2]

A Son of the Bowery

Unlike most leaders of the social gospel movement,[3] Stelzle suffered urban hardships personally. He knew firsthand the "pangs of cold and hunger experienced behind dank city tenement walls." The son of German immigrants, Stelzle's father died when he was very young. His mother tried to feed, clothe, and house the family as best she could amid the grinding poverty of the Bowery, a congested ghetto on the lower east side of Manhattan. Hunger, malnutrition, and public drunkenness were common neighborhood sights, and the Stelzles lived in an apartment with no outside ventilation. Charles went to work part-time in a tobacco sweatshop when he was eight years old; he also sold newspapers, peddled oranges, and bussed tables in a restaurant. At the age of eleven, he quit school so that he could help support the family by working all day. During his limited free time, he joined a gang of street toughs and was arrested twice.

New York City in the closing decades of the nineteenth century was a "mosaic of nations," as Stelzle aptly called it. Within its sprawling population, New York exemplified in large form all of the difficulties associated with extensive immigration and rapid industrialization—problems of health, sanitation, industrial relations, immigration, housing, unemployment, and corruption. In such an environment, the potential for delinquency was great.

Stelzle was fortunate, however, that during his adolescence he was befriended by the largehearted minister of Hope Chapel, an evangelical, inner-city Presbyterian mission. The pastor took him to ball games, tutored him three nights a week, and nurtured him in the faith. Stelzle became a member of Hope Chapel. Soon, he taught a Bible class and superintended the Sunday school. At the tender age of twenty-one, he became a lay elder of the congregation. Meanwhile, he secured a good job as a machinist apprentice in a printing press manufacturer. Stelzle joined the trade union and became familiar with the life of an industrial laborer, including the daily anxieties about such things as arbitrary dismissal and uncompensated injury.

In 1890, Stelzle received a call "to preach to workingmen." Intending to go to theological school, he quit his job and applied to several divinity schools: Princeton, Union, McCormick, and Drew. None of the seminaries would accept him, however, because of his lack of a formal high school education. Despite the rejections, Stelzle knew that he had the background necessary to succeed in ministry, for the "machine shop [had been] my training school, my university, my seminary." Confident of his call, Stelzle wrote to Dwight L. Moody, explaining his situation. Moody immediately granted Stelzle admission to his Bible Institute in Chicago.[4]

In some respects, Stelzle's religious inclinations differed from the predominant outlook at Moody Bible Institute. His preoccupation with social issues, for instance, was not shared by most of the other students; Stelzle was reminded that he "might better preach the 'simple Gospel.'" In addition, Stelzle did not respond well to the school's emphasis on receiving a "second blessing" in order to live a consecrated life of holiness. Although he was curious about "this added gift," he saw no need to obtain it for himself.[5]

Nonetheless, Stelzle considered his education at the Institute to be "a wonderful experience." His time there was extremely formative for his ministry. Despite the school's penchant for fundamentalism and the lack of social concern among some of the premillennialists there, Stelzle had a deep personal respect for many of the teachers. He especially admired D. L. Moody, whom he knew to be broadminded. Stelzle often commented favorably about Moody's effectiveness in speaking to the everyday spiritual and material needs of working people. Stelzle credited the Institute with providing him with solid teaching of the Bible and with helping him to articulate his "conservative" theological beliefs.[6]

Stelzle also appreciated the Bible Institute "for knocking out of me the conservatism in my methods of work, particularly in reaching people with the Gospel message." That is, the students and teachers at the school modeled boldness and confidence in sharing the claims of Christianity. Herein we see evidence of a paradox that was characteristic of Stelzle's career: he affirmed theological "conservatism" (adherence to traditional doctrine) while simultaneously dismissing any "conservatism" (caution or hesitancy) in regard to evangelistic methodology or the application of the gospel to social issues.[7]

Following his ministerial preparation at Moody Bible Institute, Stelzle began a series of pastorates at urban mission churches—in Minneapolis, among sawmill men and their families; in New York, at the same chapel from which he was called into the ministry; and in St. Louis, where he was ordained as a Presbyterian clergyman. In each location, Stelzle developed a wide range of religious and social activities: boys clubs, cooking classes, night schools, dispensaries, tent meetings for evangelism, "cottage meetings" for discipleship, and, in St. Louis, the largest Sunday school west of the Mississippi. Similar to the strategy taken by many city pastors during this period, Stelzle intended his congregations to be "institutional churches"—full-service facilities for poor urban folk who had limited access to social programs. Yet Stelzle ministered in other ways that were dissimilar to most Protestant clergymen, for he went outside of the church walls to speak to workingmen on their own turf—in labor halls and at union meetings.

Interpreting Workers' Needs to the Church

Stelzle became frustrated with the lack of a denomination-wide support structure for his work among urban laborers. He urged the leadership of the Presbyterian Church to develop a proactive program that would gain the allegiance of disaffected workingmen. The Board of Home Missions agreed with Stelzle's assessment of the need and, in 1903, asked him to head up the effort. By 1906 he had become the Superintendent of the Department of Church and Labor, later called the Department of Social Service. As the first Protestant social service bureau, Stelzle's department established a precedent for social agencies in many denominations and religious groups, including the Federal Council of Churches (now the National Council of Churches). During his ten-year tenure at the department, Stelzle developed many innovative programs: he collected and disseminated data to churches on the working conditions that existed in their communities; he aided congregations in starting their own workshops, employment bureaus, and unemployment telephone hot lines; he introduced the idea of setting aside an annual Labor Sunday in Protestant churches; and he encouraged the establishment of "industrial parishes," in which each congregation was responsible for the welfare of the workers in a particular factory. Somehow, he found the time to organize Sunday recreational programs for laborers, to conduct mass meetings for workers in large public halls, to hold noontime devotional meetings in factories, to write a weekly article syndicated in 150 labor newspapers, and to help formulate the famous "Social Creed" of the Federal Council of Churches.

During these years, Stelzle also became active in politics. In 1912, he made numerous speeches for the presidential campaign of Theodore Roosevelt. That same year, he accepted the nomination of Roosevelt's Progressive Party for a seat in the New Jersey State Assembly. Like William Goodell's pre-Civil War involvement in the Liberty Party, Stelzle viewed third-party politics as a means to influence American public policy on behalf of the dispossessed.

More significant than his religious and political efforts on behalf of laborers was his self-appointed role as an "interpreter" between workingmen and the churches. Since a large percentage of Presbyterian members sympathized with management's side in industrial conflicts, Stelzle felt the need to represent labor. He defended organized labor at every opportunity and tried to serve as a bridge between them and their employers.

The church, Stelzle believed, could play an important role in labor disputes by acting as an impartial mediator among the contending parties. But how, he wondered, could the church gain the trust of workers after so many years of maintaining a pro-business bias? Stelzle came up with a brilliant plan in which labor unions and local ministerial associations would exchange fraternal delegates. This plan was adopted in several hundred communities and became the accepted policy of the A.F. of L. Stelzle himself was received at the 1905 A.F. of L. convention as an official delegate representing the Presbyterian Church. He attended their annual convention for twelve consecutive years, each time giving a well-received address to the assembled body. In many cities, the ministerial delegates to local unions were viewed as chaplains to the workingmen. Consequently, just as Stelzle had envisioned, clergymen often became trusted arbitrators in industrial controversies.

Rather than antagonism, Stelzle hoped for cooperation between Protestant churches and laborers. He challenged the churches to identify with the disenfranchised of society, to "stay by the people and help them solve their problems." The church, he insisted, must not wait for working people to come to it; rather, it must go to the working people and assist them in their struggles. But due to his background as a laborer, Stelzle was sensitive to any tinges of domineering patronism in the social activity of well-meaning religious people. He urged churches to include the poor in the actual governance of their religious and social institutions, and to support his dream of an "industrial democracy," in which workers would participate in the management of their own productivity. While Stelzle's dream was typical of the idealism of American Progressivism, he tempered his idealism with a note of caution derived from his evangelical belief in the pervasive effects of human sin. Stelzle feared that the new democracy that would emerge in the United States would be dominated by a "spirit of gross materialism" instead of the self-denying "spirit of Jesus." Only the moral regeneration of character in conjunction with the transformation of society, Stelzle asserted, could stem the cultural tide of selfishness and greed.[8]

Just as Stelzle challenged the church to reach out to labor, he challenged laborers to reach out to Christ. He knew that workers had no patience with abstract "ecclesiastical discussions," but he was convinced that they would be attracted to a church that proclaimed the person and the principles of Jesus. Countering a popular misconception circulating among middle-class Protestants, Stelzle maintained that workingmen had a keen interest in religion, though he admitted that their personal behavior and bawdy "language was decidedly nonecclesiastical." Stelzle observed that laborers, "as a class, [we]re extremely conservative in matters of religion" and, therefore, should have been attracted naturally to the leading evangelical churches (such as the Presbyterians, Methodists, and Baptists)—if only those churches would have taken an interest in the plight of the workers. Most laborers were not bitter toward Christianity; they were just indifferent to organized religion because the church had nothing vital to say to them.[9]

Unfortunately, most Protestant denominations viewed urban ministry as an inconvenient burden instead of as an energizing challenge. The majority of city church ministers had been brought up in rural communities. They pastored their congregations "apart from the life of the people," basing their ministries on elaborated country church programs without a true understanding of the problems of workingmen. The Protestant denominations, Stelzle feared, had practically abandoned the city. Where his ministerial colleagues saw urban blight and the threat of socialism, Stelzle saw a "modern miracle"—"splendid, powerful, dominant." Stelzle warned his fellow clergy that if they did not become accustomed to the new urban ministry setting the Protestant churches would become irrelevant, for "the city has come to stay."[10]

The Labor Temple

Stelzle had an opportunity to put his commitments into practice when, in 1910, he founded the Labor Temple as an alternative religious "fellowship" for workers. The Labor Temple was not a conventional church; neither was it simply a religiously oriented social center. Rather, it was a "demonstration of what the Church can do in building up the whole life of the people, with special emphasis on their spiritual welfare." Stelzle took an old, declining congregation on New York's east side and initiated a completely new program intended to appeal to the average workingman. Though the ministry location was considered "the most difficult field in America," his years as pastor of the Labor Temple became the "happiest moment in [his] career as a minister."[11]

Stelzle had his work cut out for him, since the Labor Temple had to compete with saloons, brothels, and vaudeville theaters in the tenement district surrounding the church. Nearby Presbyterian congregations had already fled to the suburbs. D. L. Moody, Stelzle's prototype of successful evangelism, had tried to conduct a preaching campaign at the church a few years before, but he had been unable to attract a crowd. When Moody's assistants attempted to gather people from the street to come inside and attend the meetings, the immigrant workers of the neighborhood retorted caustically: "Who the hell is Moody?" The revivalistic style that had been the popular hallmark of nineteenth-century evangelicalism had lost its appeal among urban Americans. Stelzle realized that he would have to use untraditional methods if the Labor Temple was going to prosper. The situation demanded a new approach; he needed "a new conception of the significance of the old Gospel."[12]

It was in this context that Stelzle developed an interest in promotion and advertising.[13] Though he was extremely suspicious of capitalism as an economic system, Stelzle became enamored with the religious potential that could be derived from studying effective marketing techniques. He even wrote a book on the topic: *Principles of Successful Church Advertising*.[14] He was convinced that in order to reach the working class, religious organizations needed to learn from establishments that had already succeeded in attracting laborers, such as trade unions—and movie theaters! From the motion picture houses, Stelzle learned how to promote his meetings creatively and how to keep workers from being bored. He even installed a giant screen behind the platform, on which was flashed the words of the hymns to be sung—a predecessor of the overhead projector found at many evangelical churches today. From the trade unions (many of which met at the Labor Temple for their meetings), he obtained the idea for weeknight "open forum" discussions. Many topics were broached during these forums, including public health concerns, working conditions, and, especially, the political and economic ramifications of socialism.

Due to Stelzle's vigorous promotion, the ministry of the Labor Temple flourished. Night after night, the old church building overflowed with working men and women. The congregation began to receive national attention, including visits from dignitaries like Stelzle's friend, Theodore Roosevelt. But not all of the commentary was positive. Some traditionalists on the Presbyterian Board of Home Missions, which provided funding for the project, accused Stelzle of becoming "an out-and-out sociologist, rather than a preacher of the Gospel." Charges were brought against him at the denomination's General Assembly for allegedly teaching socialism.[15]

The charges were later dropped, and the Executive Committee of the General Assembly formally apologized for its misrepresentation of him in the church press. Nonetheless, the accusations deeply affected Stelzle. He resigned as pastor of the Labor Temple and from his position as the head of the Presbyterian Department of Church and Labor (by then called the Department of Social Service). As much as he loved the Presbyterian church, he began to doubt the efficacy of denominational structures. Given the serious social problems facing the nation, Stelzle perceived that the various churches needed to cooperate in unified concerted action. For the remainder of his active ministry (except for the War years of 1917–18, when he directed the Red Cross office related to churches and workingmen), he put his energies into public relations work on behalf of social and religious causes, especially the ecumenical efforts of the Federal Council of Churches.

The Job of an Evangelist
is a Social Job

The larger drama in which these scenes from Stelzle's life took place was the fundamentalist/modernist controversy, a conflict that had its most serious outcome in the Presbyterian church. Presbyterianism, particularly in its northern branch, had been agitated by doctrinal acrimony for several decades. An entrenched theological conservatism predominated in the church, and it came into direct conflict with the emerging liberal theology of the late nineteenth century. Several noteworthy church trials against Presbyterian liberals in the 1890s resulted in conservative control of the denominational leadership. With the conservatives wielding authority, the Presbyterian General Assembly adopted a declaration of "essential" doctrines in 1910. Other groups of conservative Christians had also developed lists of basic "fundamental" beliefs; consequently, conservatives during this period came to be known generally as fundamentalists.[16]

In and of itself, this doctrinal dispute should not have had much of an impact on Stelzle, who considered himself to be theologically orthodox. Along with the conservatives, he believed in the importance of maintaining Biblical authority and theological fidelity. Stelzle, however, had an open-minded disposition. He affirmed that "both Fundamentalists and Progressives are making a distinct contribution toward the progress and development of society and my sympathies are to a certain extent with both groups." This tolerant attitude distanced him from the exclusive spirit of fundamentalism, which was known for its defensive demeanor as much as for its particular doctrinal positions.[17]

After the turn of the century, a new development altered the theological configuration within American Protestantism, and especially within Presbyterianism: the social gospel became connected with doctrinal liberalism. In the eyes of theological conservatives, social ministry came to be viewed as a species of modernism. Among fundamentalists, "social Christianity" was identified with menacing conspiracies of all kinds. In the anxious years just before and during the first World War, conservatives associated social progressivism with the rise of German anarchism, Russian Bolshevism, and the "dangerous" liberalism of the ecumenical movement. Consequently, Billy Sunday and other well-known evangelists of the 1910s and '20s scornfully repudiated the emphasis on social issues that had been evident in the earlier revival ministries of Charles Finney and (to some degree) D. L. Moody.

Despite the tensions, Stelzle maintained a religious ethos that embraced both the new social progressivism and the older revivalistic tradition. Consequently, he was attacked by extremists on both sides. Religious and political conservatives (who were increasingly leagued with one another) accused him of spying on businessmen while in the service of organized labor. His apologetic for the Russian Revolution also soured his relationship with fundamentalists. The Russians, Stelzle claimed, were merely trying to bring in a "reign of righteousness," a cause for which Christians ought to be sympathetic. Protestant conservatives were not pleased with any of Stelzle's economic views, whether his analysis of Communism or his critique of their "smug, self-satisfied middle class" status. Indeed, the combination of religious conservatism and bourgeois complacency was particularly troublesome for Stelzle.

> We hear a good deal these days about the uprising of the radicals. But I am more concerned about the downsitting of the conservatives—those who are quite content with things as they are; who have comfortable homes, can afford to wear good clothes, are assured of enough to eat, can educate their children, and have snug little sums in the bank or in bonds which will provide for them in the future.[18]

Conservative theology and revival methods were fine, but Stelzle could not support the alliance of these religious emphases with social conservatism.[19]

Meanwhile, Stelzle also encountered severe opposition from the Left. The radical anarchist, Emma Goldman, came to the Labor Temple to refute his ministry publicly. Other Marxist-oriented labor leaders accused him of being a "tool of the capitalistic class," because he would not come out unequivocally in favor of socialism. They thought that Stelzle's continuing emphasis on personal conversion indicated that he wanted to keep workingmen satisfied in their economic condition.[20]

However, Stelzle's stress on conversion was not reactionary. Like other early social gospellers, it grew out of his conviction that individual and social regeneration were complementary. Though he encouraged the development of systemic solutions to urban social problems, he also strove to lead men and women to a relationship with Christ. Though he felt that Prohibition would not solve every social and economic problem, he supported the Eighteenth Amendment because he knew from his own pastoral experience that saloons were a menace to families. Though he supported social settlement work (especially by speaking out against conservative critics who attacked the settlements because they were not explicitly religious), he also continued to support the work of inner-city "rescue missions," because, he stated, there would always be downtrodden individuals who needed reclamation. Though he advocated radical change in the structures of social institutions, he also advocated radical change in individual moral character. Most importantly, though he proclaimed the centrality of Jesus' social message, he also believed in the importance of personal evangelism.[21]

Stelze insisted that effective evangelism in the twentieth century should be promoted by "the right kind" of evangelist—one "who has a message which is broad and deep and thoroughly evangelistic, but with a social spirit backed up by knowledge of social conditions and principles." Stelzle had outstanding credentials as this "right kind" of evangelist. At the Labor Temple, the Sunday evening sermon "was thoroughly evangelical, a straight appeal to the hearts of men." At the 1904 St. Louis World's Fair, he was placed in charge of Protestant evangelism. He travelled as a part of the preaching team for J. Wilbur Chapman (1859–1918) and other noted revivalists. Stelzle was also frequently selected as the keynote preacher for citywide evangelistic campaigns because of his ability to speak to a diversity of opinion on social and theological questions.[22]

While he advocated the preaching of personal conversion, Stelzle criticized the highly individualistic program of "traditional" evangelism. The typical privatistic approach to salvation, he contended, was limited in its appeal to "the larger life" issues that affected working people. He sought to develop a "more comprehensive" articulation of the gospel in order to touch as many as possible in the lower-class population of large cities. The "job of the evangelist," Stelzle declared, "is a social job. . . . [I]t is a bigger thing than merely urging 'individuals to accept Christ.'" Rather, the evangelist "must be interested in raising the manner of living for the entire city."[23]

Stelzle came up with the concept of a "social service revival" to further his idea of the "right kind" of evangelism. At the Labor Temple, he introduced the social service revival by inviting six prominent preachers—three progressives and three conservatives—all of whom were to speak on two subjects: "What was the purpose of Jesus?" and "What is the Kingdom of God?" As in standard evangelistic meetings, commitment cards were distributed for the congregants to sign. But these cards contained the following pledge: "I accept the purpose of Jesus—I will help bring in the Kingdom of God." This pledge, Stelzle hoped, was broad enough to include the most radical of the Labor Temple constituency as well as the most conservative Christians—"a platform upon which all could stand and have many things in common." Accepting Jesus' purpose of helping to bring in the Kingdom was a theme that was proclaimed regularly at the Labor Temple. Stelzle had the confidence to pray that "justice and happiness and brotherhood and peace may prevail throughout the whole earth."[24]

Stelzle's stress on the Kingdom of God reflected a typical theological emphasis of the social gospel. Unlike premillennial doctrine, which placed the catastrophic fulfillment of the Kingdom of God at some time in the future, the social gospellers affirmed a "realized eschatology," in which the Kingdom of God was a gradually advancing present reality as well as a future hope. This belief in a realized eschatology was in some ways a natural extension of Finney's optimistic postmillennialism. The possibility of living out God's reign on earth provided a strong impetus for addressing broad, structural social issues.[25]

Stelzle advocated the "larger righteousness of the Kingdom of God," rather than the "minor moralities of purely personal conduct" that characterized Protestant fundamentalism in the early twentieth century.[26] At the same time, his abiding conviction in the necessity of Christian regeneration indicates that he did not forget the revivalistic heritage from which he had come. As is evident throughout his writings, both of these aspects of the social service revival were essential for "the larger, fuller gospel" that was preached by and manifested in the life of Charles Stelzle.

Selections From the
Writings of Charles Stelzle

from "The Spirit of Social Unrest," (1908)[27]

[W]e must show the workingmen of this country that the Church of Jesus Christ does not stand for the present social system. It does not uphold it. It stands for only so much of it as is in accordance with the principles laid down by Jesus. . . .

Social unrest is one of the most hopeful signs of the times. Without it there can be no real progress. But this spirit of social unrest requires intelligence and unselfish direction, and it is at this point that the Church must be true to herself. I am not at all bothered about the spirit of social unrest in this twentieth century. I am not afraid of it. But it is just at this point that the Church is going to be most severely tested. . . .

What may the Church do in answer to this challenge? First of all, we need to study the problems of the people sympathetically. When our young men go to the theological seminary to study for the ministry, they study about the social life of the Canaanites, the Hittites, the Amorites, the Perizzites, the Hivites, and the Jebusites. And when they become our ministers, they preach about these very interesting people that lived so long time ago, and we listen to them with very great pleasure—that is, sometimes some of us do. But when a man studies into the social life of the people that live in Buffalo, for example, and preaches about it, some dear brother or sister will remind him that he better preach the simple Gospel, whatever that really is. I have never quite found out. To me the Gospel of Jesus Christ is as broad as humanity, and as deep as human experience. Any narrow, stingy conception of the Gospel of Jesus Christ is an insult to Jesus Christ and a slander upon Christianity. . . .

In the second place, we must stay by the people and help them solve their problems. . . . To do this we need more of the social spirit. . . . We must make the people the end of our endeavors. We must talk less about building up the Church and more about building up the people. . . .

Third, we must socialize our teaching and socially convert our membership. There is many an honest Church member who has been converted spiritually but who has never caught the social vision. He has never been converted socially. There is a great difference between the two. There are many professing Christians who believe they are keeping the first great commandment, but who are altogether ignoring the second, which Christ said was like unto the first. . . .

We need talented men and women who have caught a vision, and who will say, I shall consecrate my life to America, to the city, to the solution of these great social problems. . . . O, that God might raise up such leaders in our own beloved land who will help solve the city problem, the labor problem, the immigration problem. . . .

The Church must insist on Christ's method for changing social conditions. . . . Socialism and communism . . . are fundamentally moral problems. I would not attempt to give a definition of Socialism which would be satisfactory to every Socialist. But here is one that satisfies a good many: "From every man according to his ability; to every man according to his need." If that means anything, it means a life of service. Communism means the giving up of one's personal interest. That implies a life of self-sacrifice. . . . Each of these presupposes a strong moral character, the elimination of selfishness, and the supremacy of love. Before any of them can ever be introduced there must, first of all, be a radical change in the selfish hearts of men. To change men's selfish hearts is the chief business of the Church, and because it is true, the Church has a most important part in the solution of the social problem. This is the principle on which Jesus Christ operated, and it is because Christ operated upon this principle that His power is coming more and more to be recognized. . . .

Jesus has sent a challenge to workingmen. He is saying to them: "Follow Me. Accept My principles. Make them the controlling principles of your lives, and no power in all the universe can stop the onward march of the working-people of the world." He is also saying to employers: "Make My principles the ruling principles in your dealings with your employees and with one another."

from *The Church and Labor* (1910)[28]

The workingman does not care about the ecclesiastical discussions which occupy so much of the time of ministers' organizations, and which have to do with hair-splitting arguments that have absolutely no relationship to present-day problems. The workingman is not particularly attracted by the preaching of a liberal theology, as so many who are *not* workingmen are insisting; because, if he were, the Unitarian and the Universalist churches would be crowded by workingmen; but he has no patience with a Church of a group of ministers who are more interested in the discussion of an abstract point in theology than they are in the pressing moral problems of the twentieth century. To the average workingman, the Church seems more concerned about the sweet by and by than about the bitter here and now. The Church seems to fail in touching life in a human way. It is an institution separate and apart from life as he knows it. It does not get down to the actuality of things as he has to do with them. . . .

There may be many points of difference between the Church and Labor as to specific aims and methods, but there are enough points of agreement and a sufficient number of fundamental principles for which both stand, to warrant the Church and Labor in uniting for the purpose of carrying out a common programme. . . .

Church and Labor may cooperate, because they both believe very strongly in the salvation of society, although they may not agree in every particular as to how this salvation is to be accomplished. . . .

Church and Labor may cooperate because they both believe in the emancipation of the individual. . . . There was a time when nothing was quite so cheap as human life. Even to-day, many large employers of labor consider it cheaper to run the risk of killing their employees and paying the slight indemnity, than to go to the expense of introducing safety appliances. Labor has long been fighting for the recognition of the value of the individual human life. It has insisted that a man is of more value than a machine. . . . Jesus Christ . . . showed the world how highly God values the individual. And the Church has ever since advocated this principle.

Church and Labor may cooperate because they both believe in the care of the human body. . . . "Ye are the temples of the Holy Ghost" was the statement of the New Testament writer. . . . Labor is trying to secure higher wages and shorter hours, in order that living conditions may be improved. In such matters as sanitary reform in tenement houses and factories, in the securing of suitable social and recreative centres for the people, and in every other particular that influences the physical conditions of the masses, Church and Labor may present a united front.

Church and Labor may cooperate because they are both aiming at the development of the human soul. . . .

Because the Church and Labor have so many important things in common, it must be obvious that it would be to the advantage of both to get together so that each may become more effective. . . . The spirit of the labor movement is becoming so strongly religious, and there is so much of the social spirit developing in the Church, that it seems altogether possible that some day Church and Labor will stand upon a common platform.

from *A Son of the Bowery* (1926)[29]

I have a conviction that the right kind of an evangelist, who has a message which is broad and deep and thoroughly evangelistic, but with a social spirit backed up by knowledge of social conditions and principles, could win his way in every community in this country. He would need to be frank in his criticism of workingmen, of employers, of churches, of civic conditions, giving credit where credit was due and pointing the way to higher and better things with no visionary programs but with practical plans for utilizing the agencies in existence. Such an evangelist would win the admiration and respect of every class and creed and he would exalt Jesus and his Church throughout the community and do a large service for the people. . . .

It is a social job, this job of the evangelist—it is a bigger thing than merely urging "individuals to accept Christ." He must be interested in raising the manner of living for the entire city. He should have more of the spirit of the old prophet who dealt with the affairs of the nation and who preached about them intelligently and inspiredly. . . .

Down through the centuries men and women have fought for democracy in religion, in government, in education—they have struggled for social democracy, the democracy of the sexes, the democracy of the races, and now we are in the throes of the fight for industrial democracy. . . . Conditions throughout the whole world indicate that this is the era of the common man. Slowly but surely the masses of people are coming into their own. . . .

What shall be the attitude of the Church in this new democracy which is growing so rapidly among the people? . . .

[T]he Church above every other organization must interpret the religion of the new democracy, and this means that it must be able to interpret life in all of its aspects because our great social, economic, and political problems are fundamentally moral and religious in their nature . . . . It would seem that the Church during the next generation will have the greatest opportunity for service in all of its history. It is not a question as to whether religion is big enough to accomplish this purpose, it is rather a question as to whether the Church is big enough to apply the principles of religion to the modern situation. One of the greatest needs of the Church to-day is prophets and interpreters of life. . . .

If the Church is to make good in the modern situation, it must engage, not only in campaigns for "individual salvation," but in crusades for social salvation. . . .

What does the Church need to-day? . . . [A]bove all it needs men and women who are ready to pay the price of discipleship. . . . What does "Jesus crucified" signify if it doesn't mean service and sacrifice and suffering? The exponents of social service might well take the Cross as an emblem of their philosophy, for it is more nearly typical of what they believe than any other symbol. The deepest meaning of the Cross finds its expression in unselfish devotion to all the needs of men.

NOTES

1. To date, there have been no biographies written on Stelzle's life. The best source of information is his autobiography, *A Son of the Bowery: The Life Story*

of an East Side American (New York: George H. Doran Co., 1926), and his many other published books. Stelzle's personal papers are in the archives of Columbia University. See also George H. Nash III, "Charles Stelzle: Social Gospel Pioneer," *Journal of Presbyterian History* 50, no. 3 (fall 1972): 206–228.

2. Charles Stelzle, *The Call of the New Day to the Old Church* (New York: Fleming H. Revell, 1915), 21.

3. The standard historical surveys of the social gospel movement are C. Howard Hopkins, *The Rise of the Social Gospel in American Protestantism, 1865–1915* (New Haven, Conn.: Yale University Press, 1940); Aaron I. Abell, *The Urban Impact on American Protestantism, 1865–1900* (Cambridge, Mass.: Harvard University Press, 1943); Henry May, *Protestant Churches and Industrial America* (New York: Harper & Brothers, 1949); Robert T. Handy, ed., *The Social Gospel in America, 1870–1920* (New York: Oxford University Press, 1966); Ronald C. White and C. Howard Hopkins, *The Social Gospel: Religion and Reform in Changing America* (Philadelphia: Temple University Press, 1976); and Paul T. Phillips, *A Kingdom on Earth: Anglo-American Social Christianity, 1880–1940* (University Park, Pa.: Penn State University Press, 1996).

4. Stelzle, *A Son of the Bowery*, 52, 55–56.

5. Ibid., 56.

6. Ibid., 56–57, 128.

7. Ibid., 56–57.

8. Charles Stelzle, "The Spirit of Social Unrest," in Charles Stelzle et al., *The Social Application of Religion* (Cincinnati: Jennings & Graham, 1908), 32; *Christianity's Storm Centre: A Study of the Modern City* (New York: Fleming H. Revell, 1908), 50; Stelzle, *A Son of the Bowery*, 145, 329.

9. Charles Stelzle, *The Church and Labor* (Boston: Houghton Mifflin Co., 1910), 16–17; "The Spirit of Social Unrest," 38; *A Son of the Bowery*, 79; *The Call of the New Day to the Old Church*, 20.

10. Stelzle, *A Son of the Bowery*, 81, 280; "The Spirit of Social Unrest," 25–26.

11. Ibid., 117–33.

12. Ibid., 119, 122.

13. Susan Curtis, *A Consuming Faith: The Social Gospel and Modern American Culture* (Baltimore: Johns Hopkins University Press, 1991), 254ff.

14. Charles Stelzle, *Principles of Successful Church Advertising* (New York: Fleming H. Revell, 1908).

15. Stelzle, *A Son of the Bowery*, 171.

16. See George M. Marsden, *Fundamentalism and American Culture: The Shaping of Twentieth-Century Evangelicalism* (New York: Oxford University Press, 1980), 109–18.

17. Stelzle, *A Son of the Bowery*, 135.

18. Ibid., 134.

19. Stelzle, *The Call of the New Day to the Old Church*, 15–16.

20. Stelzle, *A Son of the Bowery*, 135.

21. Stelzle, *Christianity's Storm Centre*, 192–93, 225.

22. Stelzle, *A Son of the Bowery*, 210ff.; *Christianity's Storm Centre*, 48–49; Dale E. Soden, "Anatomy of a Presbyterian Urban Revival: J. Wilbur

Chapman in the Pacific Northwest," *American Presbyterians* 64, no. 1 (spring 1986): 55.

23. Stelzle, *A Son of the Bowery*, 216–17; *The Call of the New Day to the Old Church*, 21; *The Church and Labor*, 47–49; "The Spirit of Social Unrest," 31.

24. Stelzle, *The Call of the New Day to the Old Church; A Son of the Bowery*, 270.

25. Walter Rauschenbusch, *A Theology for the Social Gospel* (Nashville: Abingdon Press, 1978; original publication date, 1917), 224–28.

26. Stelzle, *The Call of the New Day to the Old Church*, 13.

27. Stelzle, "The Spirit of Social Unrest," 24–25, 30–32, 34–36, 38.

28. Stelzle, *The Church and Labor*, 16–17, 84–95.

29. Stelzle, *A Son of the Bowery*, 215–17, 328, 330, 334–35.

5.

VIDA SCUDDER
(1862–1954)

The Episcopal "Socialist Churchwoman": Challenging the Privileged to Live Out Christ's Great Adventure

Vida Scudder lived a privileged life. "I have never known destitution," she confided in her autobiography. "I have never been in prison. I have never missed a meal."[1] With respect to her social location, Scudder was different from most of the other people featured in this book, each of whom experienced social or economic disadvantages. Many of the spiritual commitments and justice concerns of Julia Foote, William Seymour, and Charles Stelzle, for example, were derived from their personal acquaintance with deprivation.

Rather than speaking from the perspective of impoverishment, Scudder's spirituality grew out of her restlessness with prosperity. She was discontent with the emptiness of her relatively affluent life. She felt called on by God to work for social transformation through the voluntary sacrifice of her own success and power. For Scudder, such renunciation was not a burden. It was a part of "Christ's Great Adventure," in which God provided purpose and meaning to an otherwise shallow existence.

In terms of her privileged social standing, Scudder's life situation was comparable to the affluent economic position of a large portion of U.S. society today. Thus, when she spoke about the Christian's responsibility to demonstrate a more equitable distribution of the world's goods in one's personal lifestyle as well as in one's advocacy for social justice, it behooves those of us who find ourselves in a similar place to listen up.

A Quest for Reality

Julia Davida Scudder was born in India to missionary parents.[2] Her father, David (after whom she was named), graduated from Williams College in Massachusetts, having acquired the evangelical fervor for foreign missions long associated with that school. (Following the famous Haystack Prayer Meeting of 1810, Williams became a center of Congregationalist missionary training in the nineteenth century.) Tragically, David Scudder drowned soon after the birth of his daughter. "Vida" (as she was nicknamed) and her mother returned immediately to her grandparents' home in the Boston suburb of Auburndale.

Surrounded by doting older relatives, Vida Scudder was a precocious child. She spent four years of her childhood traveling around Europe, where she exhibited an interest in cathedrals, Italian art, and medieval history. While there, she developed a lifelong Romantic appreciation for fine art and the study of the human past. By her own account, Scudder felt more comfortable among adults than among her peers and more "at home" in the Middle Ages than in her own nineteenth century. It is not surprising, then, that she also moved away from the populist evangelical piety of her Congregationalist background and toward the venerable churchly tradition of Anglicanism. At the age of fourteen, she was confirmed as an Episcopalian by the famed Boston rector, Phillips Brooks (1835–93). Brooks was a leader in the post-Civil War effort to revive Anglican spirituality in the United States.

From 1878 to 1884, Scudder attended two fine private girls' schools— the Boston Latin School and Smith College. Women's colleges like Smith were quite new at the time, and they helped to provide academic and social opportunities not often available to women in the constrained Victorian milieu of late nineteenth-century America. Despite the progressiveness of women's colleges in terms of gender roles, such institutions nevertheless continued to perpetuate a type of elitism. As Scudder phrased it, the women there were still "segregated in the prison of class."[3]

After finishing her bachelor's degree and then a master's degree in English literature, Scudder was aimless. Bored and brooding, she groped around for something meaningful to do. She felt that her life, though pleasant, had no depth. Scudder feared that she was "not a real person, but only a sort of phantom, a hollow imitation." She was trained to be able to interpret the great affective expressions of literature, but she had not experienced them herself; she was living a second-hand existence.[4]

Once again, in 1884, Scudder went abroad—this time to Oxford—in order to imbibe the intellectual and cultural wealth of England. While there, she happened to sit in on the last course of lectures taught by John Ruskin (1819–1900), the renowned social critic. Ruskin attacked the acquisitiveness associated with the laissez-faire economy of industrialized nations. He articulated an idealistic, egalitarian social theory based on his reading of the gospels. Ruskin had a large following among young intellectuals at Oxford who wished to break loose from their aristocratic status and throw in their lot with the "unprivileged." The altruistic impulse of Ruskin's disciples was demonstrated by their involvement in the University Settlements movement, in which college students lived and worked among London's poor.

Scudder listened to Ruskin's lectures week after week. Gradually, there grew within her an "intolerable stabbing pain," as the contrast between Ruskin's social vision and the "rich delights" of Oxford forced her to realize "the plethora of privilege in which [her] lot had been cast." She was awakened by Ruskin to the "reality" of economic disparity manifested by her own life and by all of Western society. Scudder came to recognize that the socioeconomic security she enjoyed ought to be a natural right for everyone.[5]

Almost immediately, Scudder's social vision and spiritual life were altered dramatically. She came to a profoundly new religious understanding, and she was determined to act on that understanding. Scudder's first attempt to practice sacrificial giving on behalf of the dispossessed resulted in her joining the Salvation Army. To some degree, Scudder's affinity for the Army can be attributed to her evangelical roots. But she was also drawn by the intensity, urgency, and ardor of the Salvation Army's faith-based commitment to serving marginalized people,[6] as expressed in their traditional sending-forth litany:

> While women weep, as they do now—We'll fight!; While little children go hungry, as they do now—We'll fight!; While men go to prison, in and out, in and out, as they do now—We'll fight!; While there is a poor lost girl upon the streets; while there remains one dark soul without the light of God—We'll fight—We'll fight to the very end!

Ultimately, the Army's individual-oriented strategy was not broad enough for Scudder. While her appreciation for the Salvation Army remained with her for the rest of her life, she became increasingly committed to the work of organizations that had more systemic strategies for dealing with social problems.

Scudder accepted the basic social gospel premise that God expects Christians to seek broad-based economic change. An individualistic or "atomistic" theology was not sufficient in an industrialized society, for it did not train Christians to recognize the impact of social entities beyond the individual. Persuaded by the ideas of her friend Walter Rauschenbusch, Scudder began to comprehend the influence of "super-personal forces." Rauschenbusch explained that there is a "kingdom of evil" composed of systemic sin operating in various social institutions. These super-personal forces of evil need to be saved just as much as individuals. According to Rauschenbusch, a "solidaristic" approach to Christian faith will see the need to work for the regeneration of society as well as for the regeneration of women and men, developing structural solutions for the resolution of structural problems. Super-personal organizations must "repent" by giving up monopolistic power and the incomes derived from legalized extortion, and then these institutions need to "convert" by coming under the "law of service."[7] Because of Scudder's strong sense that this solidaristic view of reality was correct, she spent many years of her life advocating for the development of more cooperative social institutions.

At a deeper level, though, Scudder discovered that the "vague humanitarian ardor" of social justice advocacy did not ultimately provide spiritual fulfillment for materially prosperous Christians like herself, for the culture of privilege was still left intact in their personal lives. Affluent people, she realized, needed to escape from their "class prison." Such an escape could occur only through individual relationships with disadvantaged people. Without direct, everyday connections with the poor, Scudder observed from her own life, an affluent person's existence would be "tragically cramped and incomplete." Clearly, Scudder had no patience with any kind of "armchair liberalism." Her quest for reality was resolved once she identified personally with the plight of the poor.[8]

Identification with the marginalized of society was difficult, however, given the American culture's affinity for material consumption. Scudder, along with other social gospellers, argued that capitalist consumerism undermines faith by encouraging the sins of envy, greed, pride, and indulgence. "Competitive commerce exalts selfishness to the dignity of a moral principle," Rauschenbusch declared. People cannot follow Jesus, the social gospellers reasoned, when they are weighed down by pockets that are overly full. Christian disciples were to renounce the acquisition of wealth, for their Lord admonished them not to "lay up treasures upon earth" (Matt. 6:19).

The Great
Social Settlement Adventure

With some ambivalence, the twenty-five-year-old Scudder accepted a faculty position teaching literature at Wellesley College, where she was to remain for over forty years. During this extended period of her life, Scudder's twin interests were her teaching and the work of social reconstruction. Following Ruskin's example, she was convinced that U.S. college women could start something like the University Settlements she had witnessed in Britain. In 1887, Scudder organized a group of young social activists from several eastern women's schools. They formed the College Settlements Association (C.S.A.), an organization that was active until the outbreak of the first World War.

The women in the C.S.A. did not know that a similar, soon-to-be more-famous project, called Hull House, was being planned in Chicago at the same time as their enterprise, by another social reformer, Jane Addams (1860–1935). Actually, the first settlement house established by the C.S.A., Rivington House in New York, opened before Hull House. The C.S.A. also founded two more projects, one in Philadelphia and one in Boston's South End. This last venture, Denison House, became Scudder's second home. Though these women did not realize it at the time, they were helping to formalize the beginnings of organized social work in the United States. The social settlement movement spread widely during the 1890s. Social settlements consisted of houses in tenement neighborhoods that were open day and night for education, recreation, and social services. At its peak, Denison House served fifteen hundred people per week, providing an employment bureau, English language classes, manual training, arts enrichment, children's day care, athletic programs, and drama clubs. It also became a center for trade unions, especially for women's organizations. Scudder helped to organize female workers into the Women's Trade Union League.

Though it was difficult in those Victorian days for women to shape an independent life, Scudder and her collegiate companions bucked social mores in order to support their "crazy notion." Beyond the weekday evenings and weekends that she spent at the settlement, Scudder lived at Denison House during the summer and other school breaks and, more extensively, during her sabbatical years. She modeled her "great settlement adventure" after the self-denial of St. Francis, who had "unclassed" himself by "embracing Lady Poverty." She felt that she was finally living a "real experience."[9]

Scudder's teaching prospered as her spirit of self-giving service flourished. Many of her students became active in the work at Denison House. Scudder's role, as she saw it, was to put college women in a position where they could find out about social conditions for themselves, by entering into direct relationships with people who lived in abysmal circumstances. She hoped "to rouse the coming generation to know and feel that justice could only be won at cost of a tremendous crusade of social upheaval" and settlement work would be the first step in that process.[10] As an educator, Scudder had an especially important position in which to influence young people in terms of their social conscience.

Christianity's particular contribution to the social crisis of industrialized America, Scudder was convinced, was to "encourage its more prosperous disciples to ally themselves with the tendencies which will impoverish them and handicap their power." This "strange" but "great adventure" for prosperous Christians was at the heart of Scudder's message. She knew that embarking on such an adventure was personally risky. But she also knew that anything less would result in spiritual lethargy and enervation. Jesus' standard,

Scudder determined, was that those who possessed privileges were not allowed to rest until their privileges became "the common lot."[11]

When she first volunteered at the settlement house, Scudder was fearful she would have a self-righteous attitude. Indeed, she initially felt pity toward those who visited Denison House—the typical patronizing perspective of a "slummer," a well-intentioned but often condescending person who periodically works with disadvantaged people. Gradually, however, as she spent increasingly more time living among the marginalized, Scudder came to see poor people in a new light. She ceased to view them as nameless victims but rather as individuals who were agents of their own purposeful existence. Scudder realized that social injustices could be righted "only through the co-operation if not through the initiative of those suffering from them," instead of social workers (like herself) determining the kind of activism that was most appropriate for disenfranchised persons. Due to their prophetic position within the society and their engagement in the Christian impulse to struggle for a new social order, Scudder concluded that working-class men and women were actually nearer to the "reality" she had been seeking than she was herself.[12]

Because of her direct involvement with lower-class people, Scudder became more interested in systemic strategies that addressed broad social problems. She agitated for legislation against sweatshops, child labor, and unsanitary housing. She established a visiting nurse service. She was also a delegate to the Central Labor Union in Boston, through which she was introduced to socialist concepts regarding class struggle. Subsequently, Scudder and the Denison House staff became involved in several strikes, usually by marching and picketing. In 1912, she attended and spoke at the famous Lawrence, Massachusetts, textile workers strike, a particularly ugly confrontation in which both the police (in league with the employers) and the workers committed outrageously brutal actions against one another. Scudder's participation in this strike precipitated a storm of protest and calls for her resignation among those who considered her conduct to be "unseemly" behavior for a professor at a woman's college. But no amount of criticism could dissuade her from her commitment to be a social activist in conjunction with her calling as an educator.

Drawing from the Deep Wells of Faith

Simultaneous with Scudder's social and political agitation in the secular arena was her social justice advocacy within the Church. In 1917, she helped to found The [Episcopal] Church League for Industrial Democracy, which hoped to reform American industry as a cooperative venture. Like

Charles Stelzle, Scudder was interested in interpreting the message of the gospel to workers and in interpreting workers' needs to the church. Her social activism grew out of her deeply rooted devotional life and her years of reading theology. Though not trained at any seminary, she was a very capable theologian who became the first woman to receive an honorary doctoral degree from an American divinity school.

While Scudder expressed many liberal ideas, such as the importance of emulating the ministry of Jesus and the central theological focus of the Kingdom of God, her theology was not the predictable liberalism articulated by many social gospellers. For example, Scudder viewed God both immanently and transcendently—as one who has been revealed in the time sequence of humanity yet who is wholly Other. Jesus Christ is the one who unites these immanent and transcendent aspects of God, making it possible for the divine will to enter directly into the concrete life of men and women, and also making it possible for men and women to ascend to a spiritual "union with Eternal Love."[13]

Scudder's own spiritual union with God developed as a result of her association with the Society of the Companions of the Holy Cross, a group of Episcopalian women who pledged themselves to simplicity of life, personal surrender to spiritual disciplines, the practice of intercessory prayer for social justice, and spiritual friendship with one another. Despite her despair and frustration with the institutional Church, the sustained mystical rhythm of prayer and praise to God connected with this Anglo-Catholic society provided Scudder with the spiritual resources she needed for her social activism.

Scudder was very troubled by "the menacing division between spiritual and social Christianity" in American churches. She understood and appreciated the modern repulsion toward a religious faith that had no direct connection to the needs of humanity. Nonetheless, she also knew that "social action is in the long run unmotived and perilous unless it draw[s] from deep wells of religious faith." Christianity for Scudder was both an ethical program and a spiritual power, and, as she expressed in her book *The Church and the Hour*, one aspect of the faith was not adequate without the other.[14]

Selections From the
Writings of Vida Scudder

from *The Church and the Hour* (1917)[15]

Socialists claim, and rightly, that the lack of thinking in economic terms is fatal to a sense for reality, and every Christian is under orders to learn how to think in these terms. But the business of the Church as a Church is to translate them into Christian ethics. . . . [This] means that the Church has a distinctive and difficult work to do. To probe to the quick, to trouble people, to sting them into courses of action that involve unconventionality, pluck, readiness for adventure,—that is her duty. . . .

The Church's faith in a regenerate humanity is not much in evidence just now. To regain it, she must descend into the depths of her most mystical convictions. If she can get even a wee mustard-seed measure of that faith, she can say to the mountains of class-greed and privilege, Be ye cast down and thrown into the sea. . . .

Her opportunity and her power are unique, if she will greatly dare. Her belief that the whole body of Christian people coming under her jurisdiction can and must be raised to disinterested social action, makes her mistress of a province all her own. It is her distinctive contribution to the present crisis. . . .

Her work is not to announce new economic theories, it is only incidentally to approve specific programs. It is to insist that her children sift theories uncompromisingly in the light of Christian idealism; it is above all to offer the incentive which shall draw men to try the Great Adventure of Christian living in terms of the new age. . . .

[T]he distinctive contribution of religion to the modern crisis is to encourage its more prosperous disciples to ally themselves with the tendencies which will impoverish them and handicap their power. . . .

It is spiritual suicide for the possessors of privileges to rest, until such privileges become the common lot. This truth is what the Church should hold relentlessly before men's eyes. . . .

Who can really read the Gospels and fail to find them a disturbing force? In the intimacies of Christian experience, in the very sanctuary of faith, men seeking to learn the mind of Christ discover over and over the revolutionary nature of true discipleship. . . . This has always been the case. However conservative the Church has been in her corporate and official capacity, radicals in all ages have been nursed at her breasts. But it is more the case to-day than at any previous time since the first century; for modern Christendom has awakened with a start of recognition to the historic purpose of her Master,—the establishment of the Kingdom of God on earth. . . .

[N]o Christian can remain indifferent or non-partisan toward movements for the protection of the weak. . . . It may be superficial to look to legislation as a cure for social evils, but the people who think so must be prepared with other cures. They must not be permitted to fall back on charity. . . . Neither may they dismiss the subject with the sententious remark that the one thing necessary is a change of heart. Necessary? Certainly! Change of heart is the beginning, it is not the end. Changed hearts all around, by hundreds and by thousands, are trying to express their conversion in social action. Has the Church no guidance to give to hearts when they have been changed?

. . . .This is the hour of opportunity; this is the hour of the Church. In the last fifty years she has accomplished a great preparation, by her rediscovery of the purpose of Jesus. Few and hesitant, however, have been her attempts to realize that purpose, to strive boldly, through profound labors of readjustment and reconstruction, to establish the Kingdom of God, the kingdom of love, on earth. . . .

Growing opposition threatens between two Christian schools, one humanitarian, philanthropic, even socialistic, stressing the establishment of the Kingdom of God on earth; the other mystic, individualistic, intent exclusively on the development of spiritual faculty, on the release of eternity in Time. This last school, I suppose, would not oppose temporal works of mercy when they clamored to be done; but it would take slight interest in attacking those hidden wrongs basic to the present social order. . . .

Something in most of us shares the distaste for social Christianity. And no wonder. . . . Earnest people go to Church very wistful, and what they crave from Christian preaching is not instruction about reforms. They want release for the frozen springs of will and feeling, power imparted to open the soul to the inflowing Grace of God. Too often, the modern pulpit evades their need. Too often, the modern Church seems like a great machine for the cheery promotion of social welfare, and it is natural enough if the charge is made that social service, and care for social justice, is simply that clever old enemy materialism, invading the sanctities in new disguise.

Personally, I believe that there is one way only of avoiding the menacing division between spiritual and social Christianity. I believe that the reproach of unspirituality, so often and so justly cast on social religion, is mainly due to the frequent divorce between social enthusiasm and Christian dogma; and that the special power of the Church to meet the social emergency depends on the presence within her of a large group to whom the two aspects of her heritage are alike precious and essential, and who draw their social radicalism from the Catholic faith in its wholeness. . . .

[I]t is currently assumed that revolt from dogma and zeal for social reform are mysteriously connected. . . . It is a plausible thesis, for the alliance is natural and common. All instincts of revolt sympathize while they are immature, and reaction against the accredited in religion and in society is likely to make a simultaneous appeal to the mind. . . .

The modern churches are full of people who find dogma a clog to the free spirit, and who concern themselves with it as little as may be. Let them stay, and work for righteousness. But let them recognize the value of the other school, who apprehend Christianity less as ethical program than as spiritual power, and whose firm faith in Catholic doctrine is the well-spring of revolutionary conviction. There is intimate union . . . between the Catholic faith at its fullest and social radicalism at its boldest. Strength comes to these, not from such generalized religious ideals as can be shared by Buddhist or Jew, but from the definite Gospel as interpreted by the historic Church. They leave the religion of Humanity to those without the churches, for they know a better thing,—the religion of Christ.

Religious fervor, as the past proves, is attended by a vicious danger of spiritual egotism, unless it lead to social action. But plain Christians generally know to-day, as they have always known, that for them social action is in the long run unmotived and perilous unless it draw from deep wells of religious faith. . . .

Only by cherishing the tremendous impetus to bold social action to be found in the mystical depths of dogma can the modern social movement be rescued from the half-deserved reproach of putting the body above the soul, and losing sight of the eternal in the things of time. . . .

Everyone knows that religion is undergoing a social revival. Where our fathers agonized over sins of the inner man, we lament our social crimes. Where they analyzed their relations to God, we analyze our relations to our brothers. . . .

The change of attitude may entail loss as well as gain. If it means pragmatic indifference to the things of the spirit, it means loss. If it means that anything, however lovely and sacred, supplants in the soul the supreme desire for the Living God, it cuts life at the heart-root, and though the plant may still seem green and fresh for a time, slow death is on the way. . . . The quest for union with Eternal Love is a stern and fearsome thing, and men are always seeking facile substitutes. So they try to replace this quest by a vague humanitarian ardor, press the sure truth that *laborare est orare* [work is prayer] to the point of eliminating *orare* [prayer] altogether, and make a religion out of ministering to the poor and working for social justice. When they feel the need for more contemplation, as everybody does at times, they betake them if they can to the great woods and relax pleasantly as they enjoy Nature. . . .

A condition like this is lamentable and superficial. Yet no one would lose out from religion that intense social preoccupation which is now seizing on it. For a mighty force is regenerating the whole body of the Church. The recovery of social emphasis in the spiritual life is the great means by which our age is getting "back to Christ," who in nearly all His teachings was primarily concerned with men's relations to one another. . . .

No, we cannot give up our social vision and we may not give up our ancient quest. Rightly understood, each fulfills the other. And in one special way they meet. It is the Way of Prayer, modeled on the Prayer of the Lord, the Way of Intercession. Through intercession, the old type of religion is one with the new, and aspiration rises Godward even while tenderness holds humanity in its embrace.

Intercession is the counterpart in the life within of social work in the life without.

NOTES

1. Vida D. Scudder, *On Journey* (New York: E.P. Dutton & Co., Inc., 1937), 429.

2. Along with the two versions of her autobiography (*On Journey* and *My Quest for Reality* [St. Albans, Vermont: North Country Press, 1952]), the best source of information on Scudder's life is Theresa Corcoran, *Vida Dutton Scudder* (Boston: Twayne Publishers, 1982).

3. Scudder, *On Journey*, 67.

4. Ibid., 51.

5. Ibid., 84.

6. Norris Magnuson, *Salvation in the Slums: Evangelical Social Work, 1865–1920* (Metuchen, N.J.: Scarecrow Publishers, 1977).

7. Walter Rauschenbusch, *A Theology for the Social Gospel* (Nashville: Abingdon Press, 1978, original publication date, 1917), 69–78, 110–113, 117.

8. Vida D. Scudder, *The Church and the Hour: Confessions of a Socialist Churchwoman* (New York: E.P. Dutton, 1917), 120; idem, *On Journey*, 67.

9. Scudder, *On Journey*, 128.

10. Ibid., 112, 140.

11. Scudder, *The Church and the Hour*, 36, 51.

12. Scudder, *On Journey*, 140, 149, 339.

13. Scudder, *The Church and the Hour*, 120.

14. Ibid., 65–69.

15. Scudder, 22–24, 29–30, 36, 51, 52–53, 62, 65–69, 119–23.

6.

E. STANLEY JONES
(1884–1973)
Missionary Evangelist:
Presenting a Disentangled Christ

Nothing typified the evangelical consensus of nineteenth-century American religious culture as much as the near-unanimous support that Protestant churches gave to the foreign missions enterprise. And nothing typified the religious polarization of twentieth-century Protestantism as much as the churches' vehement disagreements about the nature of the missionary task. Conservative Protestants in the years between the two World Wars asserted that Christians needed to redouble their efforts on behalf of worldwide evangelization. They did not question the historic linkage between missionary evangelism and the expansion of Western civilization. Meanwhile, many liberal Protestants during this era rejected the traditional claim that salvation was in Christ alone, and they denounced the cultural imperialism of the West. They saw the missionary's role—whatever was left of it—as cooperation with other religions in the work of social reform.[1]

As a missionary to India and as an interpreter of the missionary cause to the United States, E. Stanley Jones found himself in the middle of the liberal/conservative theological controversy during the contentious decades of the 1920s and 1930s. Unlike most of his Protestant contemporaries, however, Jones did not fall easily into one religious camp or the other. Concerning the prevailing tension between piety and justice, he insisted on articulating a faith that "by its very nature was both individual and social."[2]

Jones combined his evangelical theology with a culturally sensitive appreciation for other people. He preached a message of religious universality—that Jesus is the Savior of all of humanity—but without the hegemonic cultural pretensions characteristic of so many missionary evangelists. Jones thus presented a "disentangled Christ—disentangled from being bound up with Western culture and Western forms of Christianity."[3]

A Christian-in-the-Making

When, at the end of his life, E. Stanley Jones wrote his autobiography, he entitled it *A Song of Ascents*. Like the psalms of ascent sung by Hebrew pilgrims as they wound their way toward Jerusalem (Psalms 120–134), Jones's narrative is the account of a lifelong spiritual pilgrimage. Even at the age of eighty-three, he still understood himself to be in the midst of a continual process in which he was being formed more fully into the likeness of Jesus. When asked on which side of the twentieth-century theological divide he belonged, Jones responded that he was "not a fundamentalist or a modernist, only a Christian-in-the-making." Jones's openness to new conceptions of God's truth had a lot to do with his ability to comprehend various points of view and to learn from people of other cultures.[4]

Jones grew up in a middle-class neighborhood of Baltimore. He intended to be an attorney, but at the age of seventeen he had a dramatic conversion to Christ at an evangelistic meeting and felt called to the ministry. Due to this regenerative experience, the "center of [his] being was changed from self to Savior." His new birth became the spiritual foundation for his life. In good evangelical fashion, Jones depicted conversion as a "once-and-for-all" event, a fixed starting point. But Jones also believed that God's gift of grace was dynamic, creating an inner spontaneity regarding the things of the Spirit. Conversion was "an expanding experience to be applied to larger and larger areas of life"—a characterization illustrated in his own ministerial career.[5]

After his spiritual rebirth, Jones understood his religious faith to have a "sense of wholeness. Fragmentation was over. Life was pulled into central meanings and purposes around a single Center." By interpreting his conversion as an ever-growing experience of religious integration, Jones developed an affinity for comprehensiveness, in which various aspects of human existence—material and spiritual, personal and social—were unified into an integrated whole. Like William Goodell, Jones's religious reorientation dissolved the conventional social distinction between sacred and secular spheres. All parts of life were now considered to be sacramental.[6]

Jones's conversion moved him from dull religious routine to a "life on fire" with the love of Christ. He joined a Methodist class meeting at his home church. The close-knit fellowship of this accountability group became Jones's model for the Christian "ashram" movement that he established many years later. It was during this time of spiritual intimacy with his class that Jones was "filled with the Holy Spirit," an experience that he expressed in a similar way to Julia Foote's description of her sanctification experience. Jones felt that this second spiritual crisis event cleansed him from an enslaving bondage to the material temptations of the world and freed him to commit his total allegiance to the Kingdom of God—thereby freeing him to be able to love other people with God's love. Paradoxically then, by becoming less "worldly," Jones became more attuned to the needs of the world.

During the same year (1901), Jones's father lost his job. Everything that the family owned was taken away by the bank. For the first time in his life, Jones knew personally what poverty meant, and it became a formative experience for him. Because of the necessity to support his family, Jones worried that he would not be able to fulfill his dream of going to college. Through the generosity of relatives, however, he was able to raise enough money in 1903 to matriculate at Asbury College, an evangelical Holiness school in Kentucky.

Similar to Stelzle's training at Moody Bible Institute, Jones considered his education at Asbury to be an extremely important time in his life. Though the professors taught him in a conservative theological mold, "it was not a cantankerous conservatism, witchhunting for heresy." Rather than insisting on any sort of "rigid creedal agreement," Asbury's emphasis was on the common experience of the new birth and the fullness of the Holy Spirit. At the college, Jones recounted, he received a firm Biblical foundation to undergird his faith experience and a missionary passion for world evangelization.[7]

Indeed, it was while Jones was at Asbury that it became clear to him that he was to go to the mission field. Like thousands of other young evangelical men and women in the nineteenth and early twentieth centuries (such as Vida Scudder's parents), Jones was moved by a compelling urge to share the gospel with the non-Christian masses of humanity. Jones's individual sense of call was connected to the extensive popularity of the larger missionary movement, which, by the turn of the century, seemed on the verge of worldwide success. Due to its close association with the global expansion of European and American commercial markets, the Protestant missionary enterprise had penetrated nearly every nation of the world by 1900.

But this nineteenth-century international expansion of the gospel was not without its cost. Missionaries followed in the well-worn tracks of traders, entrepreneurs, and colonizers. The involvement of Europe and the United States in various global exploits had been fueled by many factors: the exotic desire for worldwide exploration, the capitalistic need to acquire new markets and resources, and the exploitation of various underdeveloped lands for commercial purposes. Missionaries—sometimes unwittingly, sometimes consciously—yielded to the colonial mind-set. According to many missionaries, for instance, only Western people and Western culture were considered to be wise and benevolent. Other races could share in that wisdom and benevolence, but only to the extent that they emulated the West. Meanwhile, however, some mission churches clamored to become self-governing, self-supporting, and self-propagating, though they did not receive any encouragement in that direction by their missionary patrons.[8]

Oblivious, at first, to most of this larger history of the missionary move-ment, Jones sailed for India in the autumn of 1907. He was given no ori-entation by the Methodist Mission Board, no briefing on what to do as a missionary, and no instructions on how to travel. In retrospect, all that he took with him to India was his "colossal ignorance" of the world and his be-lief that "people needed to be converted." Since he had been conservatively trained to be wary of religious innovation, he was constantly on the defen-sive regarding his theology. Jones's early theological understanding, he re-membered later, was "neat and tied up with a blue ribbon—unchanging." For eight years, Jones tried to instill this static theology into the hearts of those Indians who seemed to be the easiest to reach with the gospel—those connected to the British colonial apparatus, who themselves were at "the dying edges of an imperialistic, privileged, receding group." The profes-sional outcome of preaching such a stunted gospel was evangelistic ineffec-tiveness. The personal outcome was even worse; Jones suffered a nervous breakdown and was required to take a sabbatical back home in the States.[9]

The Right Way to Evangelize

Jones returned to India less confident in his method, but still very con-fident in his message. He was determined to find the "right way" to reach India with the gospel. This right way, he realized, was to allow India to change him, instead of expecting that he would change India. Jones referred to his new approach as "an adventure of faith"—which, interestingly, was the same expression Vida Scudder used to describe her religious experience when exposed to people who were very different from herself. Jones's en-counter with other cultures made him teachable and made his faith more dynamic. The years abroad opened Jones up to the narrowness of his orig-inal worldview and helped him to see the magnitude of all that he could learn from ethnic groups other than his own.[10]

Jones was convinced that the first thing he needed to change was the fo-cus of his evangelism. He was determined to become identified with the "real" India, the India of change, the India of the future, the India of inde-pendence. Instead of concentrating his efforts on Anglo-oriented Indians, he spent the majority of his time among the intellectual and political lead-ers who were shaping the new postcolonial India.

Through his exposure to India, Jones became aware of the enormous weaknesses of Euro-American culture. Though still appreciative of his roots, Jones offered a rather severe critique of Western civilization, one that was quite unusual for an American missionary in the 1920s. He saw Western culture as basically selfish. While the West was "great and beau-tiful on certain sides," it was "weak and ugly on others." Jones hit especially

hard on the race prejudice of the West and the political and economic exploitation of colonial lands. Most seriously, Anglo-Saxon Christianity, he
contended, was "largely individualistic and aggressive." Thus, it "lacked
those deep social meanings and social expressions which lie at the heart of
Christianity."[11]

Just as he saw the weaknesses of his own civilization, Jones became open
to the riches to be gleaned from other civilizations. In particular, he grew
to have a deep appreciation and love for India, which he considered to be
his adopted home. He hoped that the West could learn from the East, and
he was convinced that Western Christians would get a "new burst of spiritual power" when Indians accepted Christianity. Like other oppressed
peoples—such as first-century Jews and nineteenth-century African Americans—Indians were part of a "subject race." Jones believed that, because of
their experience of oppression, Indians would be able to help clarify and re-
vivify the gospel in a way that was impossible for Westerners, who were
economically affluent and spiritually complacent.[12]

Due to Jones's sense of the need for mutual interaction between the spirituality of the East and the West, he was influenced by—and became an influence on—the thought and praxis of several prominent Asian religious
leaders of the mid-twentieth century, including Mohandas Gandhi, Ra-
bindranath Tagore, D. T. Niles, and Toyohiko Kagawa. Jones's association
with Gandhi became especially significant, so much so that he wrote a book
about their relationship, entitled *Gandhi: Portrayal of a Friend.*[13] In the
book, Jones declared that his Hindu friend demonstrated "more of the
spirit of Christ than perhaps any other man East or West." Jones was particularly attracted by the Mahatma's concept of nonviolent noncooperation
(a concept appropriated later by Martin Luther King Jr. after first being exposed to Gandhi's ideas through reading Jones's book[14]). Jones accepted
Gandhi's views on nonviolence as a creative alternative to war on the one
hand and as an alternative to any kind of passive submission to systemic evil,
on the other.

Jones found so much in Gandhi that was Christlike that it was difficult
for him to be critical of the man in any substantive way. Yet Jones did admit his disappointment that Gandhi had not become a professing Christian.
Gandhi comprehended the principles of the Sermon on the Mount better
than most Christians, Jones wrote, but nonetheless he had "not come into
vital contact with the Person, Christ." In trying to sum up his paradoxical
assessment of Gandhi's religion, Jones declared that the Mahatma was "a
natural Christian rather than an orthodox one." "[H]ow shall I defend that
distinction[?]" Jones asked rhetorically. "I don't. I leave it undefended."
Gandhi, according to Jones, was a deeply Christianized Hindu, but not a
Christian.

What disturbed Jones about Gandhi's religious position was not his rejection of Christianity as much as his reason for doing so. Gandhi was not able to see Jesus as a personal Savior, Jones ascertained, because of "the cloud of racism enveloping . . . Christianity." Gandhi missed out on a first-hand experience of Jesus because missionaries and others had "held out a Christ completely covered by their Christianity"—a Christianity tied to the imperialism of Western culture.[15]

A Theological Amalgam

By the 1920s, Jones had arrived at an interesting intellectual place in his understanding of the relationship between the gospel message and human culture: he made a distinction between Christ and Christianity. The former was the Savior of all humanity; the latter the expression of religion within a specific culture. Similar in some respects to the neo-orthodox theologians of the period, such as Karl Barth and Emil Brunner, Jones perceived the in-adequacy of the religious system known as Christianity while declaring the supreme value of the person of Christ. He held to the particularity of cultures but the universality of Jesus. In this way, Jones avoided the ethno-centrism of many missionaries, yet he still affirmed the centrality of Jesus Christ inherited from his evangelical training.

Jones's religious views were an amalgam of twentieth-century theological positions: evangelical, liberal, and neo-orthodox. Evangelicalism was the most obvious theological source for his ideas, for it came from his church background and education. But Jones was also clearly influenced by Protestant liberalism. This is evident in his emphasis on the immediacy of the Kingdom of God, the importance he placed on the articulation of a social gospel, his dynamic perception of truth, his commitment to pacifism and the ideal of one world government, and his stress on the creation of Christlike character based on the model of Jesus as a pattern for humanity.[16]

On the other hand, Jones also represented the theological chastening that characterized many twentieth-century Christians—those who faced the crises of two world wars, the Cold War, global economic depression, fascist and communist totalitarianism, moral decay, and the threat of nuclear holocaust. It was difficult to remain optimistic in the face of such events. Jones knew from his experience that there was no such thing as a thoroughly "Christian nation" and, unlike Charles Finney and other ideal-istic nineteenth-century evangelicals, he had no illusions about saving the world and bringing in the millennium.[17]

Perhaps Jones's distance from the agenda of twentieth-century Protestant liberalism was most evident in his understanding of the role of Christian missions. Many American Christians of a liberal bent followed the lead of William E. Hocking (1873–1966), a Harvard philosopher. Hocking chaired an influential commission that was given the job of investigating and redefining the work of foreign missions. Hocking's final report for the commission, published in 1932, concluded that missionaries should no longer try to obtain conversions but rather should join hands with the adherents of other world religions in order to discover the common religiosity shared by all human beings. Many liberal Protestants espoused this sort of religious relativism and abandoned the evangelistic task of missions.[18]

In contrast, Jones maintained his zealous commitment to convert all people to Christ, but with an evangelistic method that was clearly different from that of most conservative missionaries. He specifically rejected the "old approaches" to missionary evangelism, such as attacking other faiths or attempting to demonstrate that Christianity fulfilled all other religions. He had no interest is such a defensive evangelistic strategy.[19]

Presenting Christ

Rather than a hard-sell or coercive style of evangelism, Jones "presented" Christ to others—in an uncomplicated manner and with as little cultural baggage as possible. Then—after his presentation—he called on the people who received the message to restate and reinterpret the Christian gospel according to their own national "genius." Each country, Jones argued, will understand the gospel uniquely. Christ will travel with the Indian people down their cultural "road." Meanwhile, Christ will travel in a different fashion down the American road, and differently yet again for another nation. By using this culturally inclusive method, Jones hoped to present Christ in a way that was "untrammeled" by Western civilization. In India and in the many other countries to which he traveled as an evangelist—Japan, Korea, Indonesia, China, South Africa, various European nations, the United States, and even the Soviet Union—Jones hoped to separate the message of the gospel from the encrustations of Western imperialism. The postcolonial world was a world of great change and disruption. The missionary's task in non-Western countries such as India, Jones declared, was simply

> to know Him, to introduce Him, to retire—not necessarily geographically, but to trust India with the Christ and trust Christ with India. We can only go so far—He and India must go the rest of the way.

Jones was convinced that "every nation has its peculiar contribution to make to the interpretation of Christianity"—ways in which each country assimilates parts of its culture with the faith. With an inclusivist mind-set that today we would term "multicultural," Jones affirmed that "those that differ from us most will probably contribute most to our expression of Christianity."[20]

Jones was especially interested in discovering the specific contributions that India could make to Christianity and then sharing those contributions with the West. Beyond his acceptance of nonviolent noncooperation, which, as noted above, he gained from Gandhi, the major offering from Indian culture that Jones assimilated into Christianity was the idea of an ashram.

An ashram is a Hindu retreat in which religious disciples seeking salvation practice disciplined corporate living under the guidance of a guru, or teacher. In 1930, Jones established a "Christian ashram" at Sat Tal in the foothills of the Himalayas, the first of hundreds that he would direct. A decade later, he transplanted the idea to the United States. Soon Christian ashrams were taking place all over the globe, and for several decades they were very popular. Christian ashrams allowed religious seekers to explore the claims of Jesus in a nonthreatening and noncoercive atmosphere of close fellowship. Each person at the ashram was known as "Brother" or "Sister," for all were seen as part of the family of God, and all worldly titles, it was explained, must disappear in God's Kingdom. It was also an essential principle of the Christian ashram that races and classes came together on the basis of complete equality.

Two Sides of One Whole—
Both Individual and Social

Jones believed that the Western emphasis on personal autonomy was an inheritance that had enriched Euro-American religion and culture, especially in the development of democracy and the importance placed on redeeming the moral character of individuals. But it also meant that the churches of the West received "only a partial expression of Christianity." Much of Protestantism failed to comprehend the essential social nature of the Kingdom of God. Thus the East, with its emphasis on the collective will of humanity, could give the West a more vital interpretation of the Kingdom.[21]

Jones knew that conservative Protestants tended to preach a "Kingdom in heaven . . . that upsets nothing on earth." Drawing from his experience in India, Jones preached a "Kingdom of God on earth and that upsets everything"—particularly the unjust structures of society. In fact, Jones believed that by stressing the concept of the Kingdom of God, it "wiped out the distinction between the individual and the social—they were two sides of one whole." Jones found the endless debates between the personal gospel and the social gospel to be specious. "I want and need one gospel,—a gospel that lays its hand on the individual and says, 'Repent, be converted,' that lays its hand on the corporate will and says, 'Repent, be converted'—one gospel, two applications." Persons and systems must both turn from selfishness to godliness.[22]

In the entirety of his life work—whether preaching to large crowds throughout the world or consulting personally with Indian leaders, whether conducting an ashram in order to lead individuals to find Christ or convening a "Round Table" discussion among politicians in order to lead nations to find peace, whether working ecumenically in the cause of evangelism or denominationally within his own Methodist Church[23]—in all of these facets of ministry, Jones sought to point simply to the person of Jesus. His extensive experiences in non-Western lands taught him to lift up the inherent possibilities of other cultures so that the whole of Christianity would be enriched by the contribution of each part. These themes are evident throughout Jones's voluminous body of writings, and especially in his two classic books, *The Christ of the Indian Road* and *Conversion*.

Selections From the
Writings of E. Stanley Jones

from *The Christ of the Indian Road* (1925)[24]

There is little to be wondered at that India hesitates about our civilization—great and beautiful on certain sides and weak and ugly on others. While some of the contacts of the West with the East have been in terms of beautiful self-sacrifice and loving service, some of them have been ugly and un-Christian. . . .

But standing amid the shadows of Western civilization, India has seen a figure who has greatly attracted her. She has hesitated in regard to any allegiance to him, for India has thought that if she took one she would have to take both—Christ and Western civilization went together. Now it is dawning upon the mind of India that she can have one without the other—Christ without Western civilization. That dawning revelation is of tremendous significance to them—and to us. . . .

[Indians are] making an amazing and remarkable discovery, namely, that Christianity and Jesus are not the same—that they may have Jesus without the system that has been built up around him in the West. . . .

[I]n all the history of Christianity whenever there has been a new emphasis upon Jesus there has been a fresh outburst of spiritual vitality. . . . Out of a subject race came this gospel in the beginning, and it may be that out of another subject race may come its clarification and revivification. . . .

Christ must not seem a Western Partisan of White Rule, but a Brother of Men. . . . [The presentation of the gospel] must not be "an incrusted Christ," to use the words of the student representative before the World's Student Conference at Peking. It must not be a Christ bound with the grave clothes of long-buried doctrinal controversy, but a Christ as fresh and living and as untrammeled as the one that greeted Mary at the empty tomb on that first Easter morning.

A Hindu puts the matter thus: "We have been unwilling to receive Christ into our hearts, but we alone are not responsible for this. Christian missionaries have held out a Christ completely covered up by their Christianity. . . ."

We . . . must acknowledge our part in the mistake and see to it that in the future India has a chance to respond to an untrammeled Christ. . . .

Jesus is universal. He can stand the shock of transplantation. He appeals to the universal heart. . . . We will give [Indians] Christ, and urge them to interpret him through their own genius and life. Then the interpretation will be first-hand and vital. If this viewpoint hurts our denominational pride, it may help our Christianity. . . .

The Christian church in its sanest and most spiritual times has fixed upon the person of Jesus as the center and real essential of Christianity. But as his teaching and life goes through each national genius it receives a tinge from the life through which it passes. . . .

The Anglo-Saxon inheritance has deeply influenced Christianity. . . . Christianity coming in contact with this social inheritance has been expressed largely in terms of self-reliance, aggressiveness, and individual freedom. . . . This is certainly an inheritance that has enriched, but it has also given only a partial expression of Christianity and has lacked those deep social meanings and social expressions which lie at the heart of Christianity. Protestantism with its love of individual liberty flourished in this atmosphere. But as someone has said, "Protestantism in breaking up the idea of a universal church came near losing the idea of our universal humanity." We are just now trying to counteract that bad effect by the message of the social application of the gospel. . . .

Every nation has its peculiar contribution to make to the interpretation of Christianity. The Son of man is too great to be expressed by any one portion of humanity. Those that differ from us most will probably contribute most to our expression of Christianity. . . .

In th[e] clash of ideas and ideals we have not been called upon to modify a single thing about [Jesus]. We are called upon, with deep insistence, to modify our civilization, our church, ourselves—everything, except him.

from *Conversion* (1959)[25]

Many are converted to church membership, which is good, but not good enough. . . . Others are converted to the hope of escaping hell and getting to heaven. This is involved in conversion, but if it is made the end in view of conversion it will also let you down. If you pursue heaven as the goal, it will elude you. . . . Others still are converted to escape from unhappiness, from ill-health, from failure. These are included in conversion, but if the emphasis is on these, they too are inadequate as life goals, for if pursued for themselves they will slip through your grasping fingers. They are by-products of something bigger and greater. What is that bigger and greater?

In giving this bigger and greater Jesus Himself was never bigger and greater. With unerring insight He pointed to the Kingdom of God as that to which the converted are converted. Conversion, the new birth, is set within the framework of the Kingdom of God. . . .

The Kingdom of God is the be-all and the end-all of repentance, conversion, and the new birth. That is of the utmost importance for they introduce you to the most amazing individual and social fact of the universe—the Kingdom of God. . . .

The Kingdom is God's Absolute Order confronting this relative order of man with an imperious, "Repent, be converted, be born again and through these accept and live according to the Kingdom."

Note that you do not "build the Kingdom," as the emphasis was a generation ago and still lingers on in anemic vocabularies—you "receive the Kingdom." "Let us be grateful for receiving a kingdom which cannot be shaken" (Heb. 12:28.) "Building the Kingdom" depicts the unsurrendered self thinking it can build the Kingdom by its own efforts. But "receiving the Kingdom" depicts the surrendered, receptive self with emptied hands accepting God's gift of grace, forgiveness, conversion, new birth, and—this is the point—introducing him to the most exciting fact of the universe, the Kingdom of God. . . .

Since conversion introduces one to the Kingdom of God as an Absolute Order demanding a total obedience in the total life, individual and social, it determines the content of that conversion. The content of that conversion is personal. It attaches the individual to the personal Christ in supreme loyalty and love. He is the gateway into that Kingdom. The fact is that the Kingdom is embodied in Him. . . . He is the Kingdom personalized. So in conversion you are not attached primarily to an order, nor to an institution, nor to a movement, nor to a set of beliefs, nor to a code of action—you are primarily attached to a Person, and secondarily to these other things. . . . The center of conversion is the belonging of a person to a Person.

Embodied in that Person is a Kingdom, so when you have relationships with that Person you have relationships with that Kingdom. But the nature of that Kingdom is social—the whole of life, individual and social, comes under its sway. It demands a total obedience in the total life. Entrance into the Kingdom is personal, but the nature of that Kingdom is social. So the content of conversion is by its very nature both individual and social, not now individual and now social—it is both at one and the same time. That is according to the very make-up of the individual as an individual. He is not now individual and now social. He is both at once. "To be is to be in relations." You cannot "be" without being "in relations." As man by his very nature is at once personal and social, so conversion by its very nature is both. The division between an individual and a social gospel is gone. To separate them is to separate what God joined in the Incarnation when the Word became flesh.

Since conversion converts to the Kingdom of God then the area of operation for conversion is the whole of life—individual and social. Jesus gave the content of the Kingdom when He announced His manifesto in the little synagogue at Nazareth in the very beginning of His ministry, "The Spirit of the Lord is upon me, because he has anointed me to preach good news to the poor (the economically disinherited). He has sent me to proclaim release to the captives (the socially and politically disinherited) and recovering of sight to the blind (the physically disinherited), to set at liberty those who are oppressed ("bruised"—K.J.V.—the morally and spiritually disinherited, those who have bruised themselves upon the moral and spiritual laws), to proclaim the acceptable year of the Lord (or the Lord's year of Jubilee—the Year of Jubilee in which all slaves were freed, all debts cancelled and all land redistributed and the nation began on a basis of a close approximation to equality . . .)."

Here was a reconstruction that would remake the economic, the social and political, the physical, the moral and spiritual, and the collective. . . .

A living, growing conversion is conversion taking in greater and greater areas of life. . . . [D]edication to the Kingdom . . . will bring all life into coherence and goal and give it a sense of mission. The false division between the secular and the sacred will be wiped out. The whole of life will be sacred, because used for sacred ends—Kingdom of God ends. . . . Conversion is conversion to the Kingdom of God.

NOTES

    1. David J. Bosch, *Transforming Mission: Paradigm Shifts in Theology of Mission* (Maryknoll, N.Y.: Orbis Books, 1991), 297, 304.
    2. E. Stanley Jones, *A Song of Ascents: A Spiritual Autobiography* (Nashville: Abingdon Press, 1968), 151.
    3. Jones, *A Song of Ascents*, 110.
    4. Ibid., 17, 44.
    5. Ibid., 28, 41.
    6. Ibid., 29.

7. Ibid., 67.

8. Stephen Neill, *A History of Christian Missions*, 2d ed. (New York: Penguin Books, 1986), 207–21; Bosch, *Transforming Mission*, 290–96, 307.

9. Jones, *A Song of Ascents*, 80–82.

10. E. Stanley Jones, *The Christ of the Indian Road* (New York: Grosset & Dunlap, 1925), 22; *A Song of Ascents*, 91, 108.

11. Jones, *The Christ of the Indian Road*, 14–16, 56, 201–2.

12. Ibid., 19.

13. E. Stanley Jones, *Gandhi: Portrayal of a Friend* (New York, Abingdon-Cokesbury Press, 1948).

14. Jones, *A Song of Ascents*, 260.

15. Jones, *Gandhi: Portrayal of a Friend*, 59–61; *A Song of Ascents*, 131–35; *The Christ of the Indian Road*, 31.

16. Jones, *The Christ of the Indian Road*, 40.

17. Jones, *A Song of Ascents*, 225.

18. Neill, *A History of Christian Missions*, 418–19; Bosch, *Transforming Mission*, 326; William Ernest Hocking, *Re-Thinking Missions: A Laymen's Inquiry After One Hundred Years* (New York: Harper & Brothers, 1932).

19. E. Stanley Jones, *Conversion* (New York: Abingdon Press, 1959).

20. Jones, *The Christ of the Indian Road*, 31, 203–4, 223.

21. Ibid., 202.

22. Jones, *A Song of Ascents*, 125, 151.

23. Jones was elected bishop of the Methodist Episcopal Church in 1928 but declined the office so that he could remain in India.

24. Jones, *The Christ of the Indian Road*, 14–15, 16–18, 19, 27, 31, 32, 39, 199, 201–02, 204, 219. Copyright 1925, Mrs. E. Jones Matthews. Used by permission of the publisher, Abingdon Press.

25. E. Stanley Jones, *Conversion* (New York: Abingdon Press, 1959), 240–45, 249. Copyright 1959, Mrs. E. Jones Matthews. Used by permission of the publisher, Abingdon Press.

7.

CLARENCE JORDAN
(1912–1969)
Creator of The "Cotton Patch" Gospel:
Building Biblical Community

Every year, thousands of Habitat for Humanity volunteers construct low-cost, interest-free houses for poor people throughout the United States and in other countries. Former President Jimmy Carter and former Atlanta mayor Andrew Young, among other public figures, have lent their clout and their manual labor to the cause. Meanwhile, a generation of Christians discovered a fresh and relevant way to read the New Testament through the "Cotton Patch" rendition of the scriptures, a version of the Bible that is translated into the vernacular of the American South. Other socially engaged Christians have found inspiration for their critique of U.S. racism, materialism, and militarism from a southwest Georgia experiment in communal living known as Koinonia Farm. What do these various projects have in common? Each innovative initiative came from the creative mind of Clarence Jordan.

Jordan combined the evangelical warmth and Biblically centered faith of his Southern Baptist background with an ardent commitment to social justice and interracial unity. His careful study of the New Testament convinced him that the early church's model of Christian community is still applicable for today. Consequently, he acted on his beliefs by trying to live out the first-century pattern of Christian fellowship in twentieth-century Georgia. Though rejected and tormented by his white neighbors, Jordan found a responsive local constituency among disenfranchised African Americans. He also found a responsive national constituency among disillusioned Christians of all races. Through Jordan's life and witness, men and women heard a redemptive Word in the midst of the cultural captivity of the American churches in the 1950s and 1960s.

A Child of the South

Clarence Jordan knew from his earliest memory that he disagreed with the way in which African Americans were treated—a peculiar attitude for a white boy in the segregationist South of the early twentieth century. Except for that one idiosyncrasy, Jordan had a rather unremarkable childhood growing up in the small Georgia town of Talbotton.[1] His father owned two local businesses: a general store and a small bank. As with many rural southerners, the Jordan family's social life centered around the Baptist church of the community, including their attendance at weekly worship and Sunday School, church suppers, missionary conventions, and periodic revival services.

During an August revival meeting when he was twelve years old, Jordan made an evangelical confession of faith, was baptized, and joined the church. Only two days later, sitting again at the revival, Jordan was shocked when he recognized one of the men singing fervently in the choir. It was the warden of the county prison. Since the jailhouse was located directly behind Jordan's house, he witnessed many of the things that went on there. He had made friends with the prison cook and visited with some of the prisoners when they were allowed to sit outside in the yard. Jordan knew from his observations and conversations that the man singing so piously at the revival was the same man who beat black prisoners with whips and stretched their bodies in a primitive rack-like structure. Jordan was deeply disturbed by the incongruity of the warden's actions at church and at work. Even at this early age, Jordan knew that the Christian faith to which he aspired differed radically from the hypocritical religion he observed around him. He was particularly bothered by white America's acceptance of racial oppression and its overemphasis on worldly possessions.

As a teenager, Jordan dreamed of becoming a lawyer in order to bring justice to jails like the one in his home town. By the end of high school, though, he had decided to become a scientific farmer, for he realized that most poor people were "not stretched by ropes, but by hunger, by oppression." He hoped to learn how to help African American sharecroppers get more output from their hard work—and perhaps be able to purchase and cultivate their own farms.[2]

In 1929, Jordan enrolled at Georgia State College of Agriculture in Athens. He did very well academically. Extracurricularly, he joined the Reserve Officers' Training Corps and the staff of the student agricultural newspaper. But as Jordan was about to complete college, two things became clear in his mind: first, he was called to be a preacher; and, second, he was unable to reconcile his military training with Jesus' teachings about nonresistance, as recorded in the Sermon on the Mount. He resigned his ROTC commission and applied to seminary.

The next fall, Jordan moved to Louisville, Kentucky, in order to attend Southern Baptist Theological Seminary. It was 1933, during the worst period of the Depression. His father's businesses had failed, and, financially, Jordan was now completely on his own. To help pay his way, Jordan took a job as a part-time student pastor. Several lifechanging decisions were made while he was a divinity student. He met and married his wife, Florence Kroeger, an assistant librarian at the Seminary. He also decided to pursue further graduate studies at Southern Seminary in the field of New Testament, in order to have a stronger Biblical foundation for his vocation of service among the poor.

While studying for his Ph.D., Jordan was employed at a Baptist mission in Louisville that worked with inner-city African Americans. He insisted that blacks share in the governance of the mission, and he labored tirelessly to provide opportunities for interracial fellowship among black and white Christians. When he wanted to transfer his church membership to the African American congregation that he was attending, a storm of protest arose from the white Baptists who paid his salary at the mission. Jordan agreed not to join the church, but he confided in his journal that his Bible-touting white brethren might as well have torn "out of the New Testament all those pages which proclaim the universality of the Christian brotherhood and which so terribly upset our complacent social traditions."[3]

Meanwhile, through his work at the mission, Jordan sought to involve white seminary students in the African American churches of Louisville. These students looked to Jordan for spiritual direction, and he met with them regularly for Bible study and discussion. He shared with them his evolving ideas about pacifism, racial equality, and the radical stewardship of material resources. When this group of serious-minded student activists wanted to identify themselves with a name, Jordan suggested the Greek term *koinonia*, based on a passage from the fourth chapter of Acts that described the way in which the early church community shared all things in common.

Looking Anew at the Word of God

According to those who knew him, Jordan had a "love affair with the Bible," a natural result of his Southern Baptist upbringing. Southern Baptists affirm that the authoritative Word of God should command the full allegiance of Christian believers. The inspired scriptures are considered to be completely trustworthy and ought to be the primary source of daily inspiration for faithful living. Jordan took this view of Biblical authority so seriously he ended up critiquing his fellow Southern Baptists by their own professed standard.[4]

Jordan began to wonder whether Southern Baptists actually examined the

gospels that they claimed to follow. He doubted whether a believer could im-
itate Christ without diligently studying the scriptures. "You can't know
Jesus," Jordan wrote, "without the Bible. All the knowledge we have of him
originates there."[5] Consequently, in his seminary education, Jordan focused
most of his course work on studying the Bible, especially the Greek New Testament. He wanted to get at the nub of the gospel so that he could be a faithful disciple. Because Jordan accepted the Bible as the "Holy inspired Word
of God," he used it as his theological and ethical guidebook in all matters.[6]

Although Jordan had a very high view of the authority of the scriptures,
he did not conform to the typical conservative Baptist method of understanding the Bible. While revering the Biblical message, Jordan did not interpret the text in a literal fashion. At Southern Seminary in the 1930s, Jordan
was exposed to the historical-critical method of exegeting the scriptures. This
was no rampant skepticism, however, for his Bible teachers were committed
evangelical Christians. Rather, Jordan's professors freed him up to investi-
gate the human element involved in the scriptures while still maintaining a
deeply respectful attitude toward the text. He learned to look at the Bible as
a living document, in which finite human language was used by the Spirit to
express divine truth. Since language is, by its very nature, figurative and dynamic, the words of the Bible were to be seen as a means of ascertaining God's
Word for humanity. The scriptures were not intended to be manipulated by
legalistic proof-texting, as often occurred among fundamentalists.

Through his experiences, especially through his ministry situation—in
which he worked among poor people at the same time that he was studying the New Testament—Jordan began to look anew at the Word of God.
Almost by accident, he stumbled upon the action-reflection model of
Biblical interpretation that is now commonly used among Latin American
Christian Base Communities. The fresh understanding that he found
in the New Testament differed from the privatistic Biblical message
often stressed by his white contemporaries. Several overarching scriptural
themes became apparent to Jordan as he grappled with the text in the context of racial oppression.

First, Jordan discovered in the New Testament the central theme of
God's incarnation. God was present in Jesus and continues to be a present
reality through the Spirit in the midst of the human experience. "The incarnation of Jesus is not a point, but a process," Jordan wrote. God's indwelling was not an isolated moment in history in which God came to earth
and then returned to heaven, but an "invasion" which continues in today's
society. God has come to participate in our earthly existence. Just as Jesus
made righteous action for needy people the focus of his life, so we who
claim to follow him must express our belief, through the power of the
Spirit, by our daily actions on behalf of a hurting humanity.[7]

Related to this all-embracing scriptural theme of incarnation was Jordan's stress on the Kingdom of God, which he saw as central to Jesus' proclamation as recorded in the New Testament. The Kingdom, according to Jordan, was simply a corporate expression of God's incarnation. Jordan's conception of the Kingdom of God was similar to the image of the Kingdom that had been emphasized by Protestant liberals for over a generation, but he did not obtain his interpretation from liberalism. Rather, it was due to his Baptist habit of sticking closely to the actual words of the Bible that caused him to discover the importance of this New Testament concept.

Although Jordan's views on social issues were considered to be liberal, he was conservative in many ways. His strict adherence to the meaning and trustworthiness of the scriptural text, for instance, indicated a rather traditional view of the authority of the Bible—although it had extremely radical implications. Throughout the history of the church, those who have taken the Biblical message seriously have been some of its most effective reformers. Jordan also held to a conventional evangelical view of the pervasiveness of sin and the inability of people to overcome their captivity to sin without the redemptive power of Christ.

The significance that Jordan placed on Christ's actions on our behalf led to his call for a radical discipleship—another major theme that he perceived in the New Testament. He taught that the life of faith has a fundamentally transformative nature that ought to set the Christian apart from the ethical compromises of the world. This active faith will result in concrete praxis on behalf of the poor and disenfranchised of society. One who follows Jesus in such a discipleship, Jordan realized, must be willing to endure the reproach that the Savior himself experienced.

The power to be able to withstand the opposition of the dominant forces in society would come from the support of the community of faith. Thus, Christian fellowship, or *koinonia*, was another essential scriptural theme lifted up by Jordan. In particular, he viewed several specific passages from the book of Acts describing the early church community as the "authoritative precedent" for the manner in which fellowship should be evidenced by present-day Christians.[8] For instance, Jordan reworded Acts chapter 4 to characterize the way in which God intended church people to be "bound together . . . by the sense of community, by the common meal and the prayers." In the first century, "the whole company of believers stuck together and held all things common."[9] The obvious implication, Jordan declared, was that contemporary congregants should emulate the early church pattern.

Koinonia Farm

Jordan had very specific ideas as to how *koinonia* was to be demonstrated in the lives of Christians. But how, he wondered, could these potentially revolutionary ideas be manifest within the racist, consumerist society that existed all around him? Jordan determined that only by establishing an alternative Christian community could God's vision be expressed. Thus was born Koinonia Farm, an experiment in Christian communitarianism that began in 1942 near the southwest Georgia town of Americus.

Religious communitarianism has had a long history in the United States, from the Ephrata community of the eighteenth century, to the Zoar, Oneida, Amana, Brook Farm, Hopedale, and Shaker communities of the nineteenth century,[10] to various utopian socialist experiments of the twentieth century. Yet Koinonia Farm did not consciously draw from the experience of any of these previous communities, and it preceded by two decades the 1960s' resurgence of interest in intentional communal living. Only after Koinonia was firmly established did the community make contact with two of the older communitarian groups in America, the Hutterites and the Bruderhof.[11]

What seems to be more closely related to the factors leading to the original organization of Koinonia Farm was the interest in radical discipleship that developed during and after the second World War among a number of progressive Southern ministers. For example, some Baptist preachers, such as Carlyle Marney and Will Campbell, summoned their colleagues to examine Southern culture critically in light of the thoroughgoing ethical claims of the gospel. Other Southerners founded interracial ministry projects. These ventures were, in some ways, similar to Koinonia Farm, particularly Miles Horton's Highlander Folk Life Center in Tennessee, John Perkins's Voice of Calvary ministry in Mississippi, and Gordon and Mary Cosby's Church of the Savior in Washington, D.C.

Each of these Christian leaders sensed that Southern white churches—and American churches more generally—were held in a kind of cultural captivity to the systemic forces of racism and materialism in U.S. society. As heirs to the "spirituality of the church" doctrine, most twentieth-century Southern congregations did not take responsibility for relating the comprehensiveness of the Christian message to the social order. Typically, clergymen preached that personal spirituality alone was the province of the Church; Christians were not to meddle with political, economic, or social questions. Consequently, in the words of one historian, white church people in the South became "enslaved to the traditional spirit of color caste," unable to challenge the status quo with the radical demands of Jesus' message.[12]

The cultural captivity of post-World War II American churches was more than just a Southern problem, however. Though the "baby boom" after the War resulted in enormous numerical gains for Christian denominations in the United States, not all was well with Protestant churches. A number of religious figures in the 1950s and 1960s decried the capitulation

of the churches to the prevailing middle-class complacency regarding social issues. The 1950s, in particular, was a period when fast-growing suburban congregations ignored the problems and concerns of urban America.
In the face of this withdrawal from the needs of America's poor, many concerned men and women longed for a renewed sense of Christian community and responsibility among the churches of the nation.[13]

Even as congregations expanded their membership rolls, their budgets,
and their physical plants during the postwar period, a vague uneasiness settled in among some Christians. Jordan was able to express this spiritual discontent in a plainspeaking way that was clearly understood by many
American Protestants. He became convinced that although church organizations may be highly successful by worldly standards, they may really be
in decline according to the standards of God's Kingdom. He objected to
churches that had so merged with the surrounding secular society that they
had lost their distinctiveness and had forgotten their true calling.

Determined to make a difference by providing a model of true Biblical
fellowship, Clarence and Florence Jordan, along with another couple,
bought a four-hundred-acre tract of land and started to cultivate crops.[14]
Though Clarence had studied agriculture, none of the young idealists had
actually managed a farm. Their lack of practical experience was so great that,
according to an oft-repeated story, during planting season Clarence stood
on the roof of the barn in order to figure out what his neighbor farmers were
doing next. Despite this inauspicious beginning, a number of persons—both
white and black—came to join the Koinonia experiment in communal living. About sixty people resided on the farm by the early 1950s, voluntarily
banding together in order to live out their understanding of God's will.

Over the years, certain expectations evolved for those who became a part
of Koinonia Farm. First, reflecting his evangelical background, Jordan
stressed the essentiality of spiritual rebirth leading to a repentant change of
behavior and total surrender to God. As a mark of this spiritual surrender,
all members of Koinonia were expected to share their personal resources
with the community. These common goods were then distributed among
the members according to need.

Jordan believed that Americans overemphasized the importance of material possessions, often leading to an addictive and spiritually destructive
attitude of greed. In contrast, Christians in the early church, according to
the book of Acts, did not consider "their property to be private, but all
things were shared," a principle that Jordan intended to emulate at
Koinonia.[15]

Another distinctive expectation of community life at Koinonia Farm was
the full racial equality of all persons. Jordan never intended to start an organized movement for racial integration; he simply wanted to witness to the
world the inclusive nature of the Kingdom of God, which seemed patently

evident to him in his reading of the Bible. As Jordan studied the New Testament, it became clear to him that Paul's demand that the early church accept Gentile believers of a different ethnic background was directly applicable to the ethnic inequalities of religious life in the United States, in which African Americans were segregated from the larger community of faith. Jordan's paraphrase of Ephesians contains this interpretation of Paul's inclusive intent for the Church: those "who once were . . . segregated are [now] warmly welcomed into the Christian fellowship."

Typically, Jordan's understanding of racial reconciliation centered on the work of Jesus Christ. It was Christ, Jordan proclaimed, "who integrated us and abolished the segregation patterns which caused so much hostility. . . . [B]y his sacrifice on the cross he joined together both sides into one body." Jesus' self-giving love provided the building materials for an inclusive church and now "all are a vital part of God's spiritual dwelling place."[16]

Not surprisingly, Koinonia Farm fell victim to several spasms of violence from local segregationists. It should be remembered that Jordan and his colleagues practiced their principle of interracial fellowship from the very beginning of the community in the early 1940s—long before the highly visible Civil Rights' milestones such as the 1954 Brown v. Board of Education Supreme Court decision ending legalized segregation and the 1955 Montgomery Bus Boycott. They challenged one of the bedrock cultural conventions of the rural South, and they paid for it by receiving unwelcome visits and harassment from the Ku Klux Klan. For years, they were boycotted by most local, white-owned businesses, and they were also ejected from the membership of the Southern Baptist church in the nearby town of Americus.

Another controversial principle was the community's opposition to all forms of violence. They took a consistent stand for conscientious objection from military involvement, a stand which they maintained through World War II, the Korean War, and the Vietnam War. They also held a strong position against nuclear weapons of mass destruction.

More than just pacifism, Jordan and the other members of Koinonia were engaged in a proactive program of "waging peace," similar to Martin Luther King's attitude of "nonviolent action." Again, these activities were spiritually derived, based on their understanding of the redemptive love of Christ. Such nonviolent activism in the 1950s' McCarthy era of anticommunism brought the community even more notoriety than their integrationist practices. During the Red Scare of the mid-1950s, federal and state government agents questioned their patriotism and charged that Koinonia was a communist front. From 1956 to 1958, the members of Koinonia Farm received death threats, physical intimidation and beatings, and the bombing of their roadside produce stand. These events effected an enormous emotional toll on the community, and by 1960 many people had left.[17]

The Challenge of the 1960s

The number of people at Koinonia Farm waxed and waned over the years, but Jordan's commitment never wavered. Like many intentional Christian communities (for example, Sojourners, Patchwork Central, Church of the Savior, Reba Place Fellowship), Koinonia Farm has ceased to function in its original form, but it continues to live on through a variety of other social ministries. Ironically, though the 1960s was a period of social idealism, it was a difficult time for Koinonia. The Civil Rights struggle had moved on to more visible locales. Strain developed between the individual family units and the larger community "family." The distribution of community goods based on need proved to be a difficult concept to administer equitably.

Jordan, frustrated with some of the aspects of intentional community living and longing for a more aggressive expression of the vision within him, explored the possibility of a new direction for Koinonia Farm. Providentially, just at this time, a talented young attorney and businessman named Millard Fuller came to the farm and gained Jordan's confidence. Together, they came up with the concept of Koinonia Partners, a ministry in which homes would be built for the poor people of the Americus area. Money and labor from relatively prosperous U.S. Christians who wished to contribute to the cause would be channeled through the Fund for Humanity, which made non-interest-bearing loans to those in need. In this manner, the "spiritual dwelling place" that Jordan spoke of so profoundly took tangible form in the construction of temporal dwelling places for God's people, especially the marginalized and disenfranchised.[18]

Tragically, Jordan died suddenly of a heart attack just before the completion of the first home built by Koinonia Partners. His death, on October 29, 1969, occurred somewhat symbolically just two months before the end of the idealistic 1960s. But Jordan's death did not stop the dream, for the seeds of his ministry eventually became the international program of Habitat for Humanity. Jordan's witness also helped to shape the Biblically inclusive worldview of many Americans of his generation, including none other than a future president of the United States—Jimmy Carter—who happened to have been a Georgia neighbor to Koinonia Farm. Carter has written that Jordan's concern for racial reconciliation and the alleviation of poverty was a primary influence on his own attempt to unite spirituality and social action.[19]

We must not forget another lasting outcome of Jordan's ministry. As part of his soul-searching during the 1960s, Jordan returned to the original source of his inspiration, the New Testament. The mid-twentieth century had witnessed an explosion of interest in the Biblical text, and many new translations and paraphrases were produced. Jordan hoped to build on this interest by writing down his own rendition of the scriptures in a bold way that would make them come alive. He decided to incorporate his many years of Biblical study into a new interpretation of the New Testament.

Jordan composed his translation in the simple everyday language of the rural South. Like the Southern tradition of storytelling, he wrote in an approachable, easygoing style. This "Cotton Patch" version made the Bible more applicable to the concerns of socially conscious Christians. For example, taking his cue from the Civil Rights movement and the antiwar movement, Jordan reworded the Kingdom of God as "the God movement"—God's spiritual organization for accomplishing radical change. Immediately, Jesus' concept became newly relevant to a whole generation of young activists. In this way, Jordan's contemporary designations of various Biblical ideas provided a fresh reading of the scriptural imperative to live out God's Word in the world. And Jordan's colloquial way of paraphrasing the Gospel message—along with the example of his life—still resonates today.

Selections From the
Writings of Clarence Jordan

from "Christian Community in the South," (1956–1957)[20]

The phrase most frequently upon Jesus' lips was "the Kingdom of God." It was the center of all his preaching and teaching. . . .

The citizens of the Kingdom were the poor in spirit. They were those who were persecuted for righteousness sake, and who rejoiced when they were reviled, denounced, and slandered for something beyond themselves. They had no possessions, yet it was the Father's good pleasure to give them the Kingdom.

To enter this Kingdom was to be saved, to find eternal life.

The most likely candidates for citizenship were those least bound by tradition, custom, and creed, who were flexible enough, and willing enough, to go through a complete metamorphosis of mind and soul, a process called "repentance" in the New Testament. . . .

What was this Kingdom of the Reversed Social Order, this revolutionary Kingdom of God? . . .

God's Kingdom . . . was his family, the family of the Father. The citizens were sons, and therefore brothers.

The early Christians felt this sense of kinship very deeply. They were "one in Christ Jesus." They were "the body of Jesus." There was no "middle wall of partition" between them. Differences between Jew and Gentile, Greek and barbarian, were dissolved.

Their newly-found spiritual life revolved around the church, or brotherhood, which made the love-fellowship a reality.

Such a deep fellowship was called a "koinonia." It is the Greek word used in Acts 2:42 and is there translated simply "fellowship." This koinonia, or fellowship, is then described in the verses which follow (Acts 2:43–47) and again in Acts 4:32–35. It is obvious that this is a description of life in a family. It is the way the Father's children live together.

Wishing to realize anew the intensity of this fellowship, a group of nearly sixty men, women and children are living together at Koinonia Farm, in southwest Georgia near Americus. We have come together from many denominations, occupations, and sections of the nation. Some of us are white, some negro. Our education ranges from illiteracy to Ph.D. Our economic backgrounds are from middle-class to poor. We come from both farms and cities, from North and South. . . .

[I]t might be well to examine some of the spiritual beliefs which hold [the community] together. First, we believe that any commitment to Christ is a total one, involving surrender of self, vocation, possessions—everything. It transcends all human commitments or loyalties and, like marriage, is for better or for worse.

While this commitment cannot be equated with our relationship to Christ's church-community, neither can it be separated from it. Christ apart from his church is the Word apart from the flesh. The two belong together. We there make our surrender to Christ a concrete, objective act by turning over everything, including ourselves, to his church-community, or koinonia.

This community of spirit, then, quite naturally produces community of goods. None of us says that anything is his own, but we hold all things common. All income, from any source whatsoever, goes into a common treasury. All property is held by the community, which is a legal corporation. This principle of common ownership characterizes any human family where a real love relationship exists, and we feel that a family of the Father should do no less.

Another principle which always exists where love prevails is distribution according to need. Jesus taught us to love one's neighbor *as* one's self, which means that no one is to place himself above, or below, his brother. He will ask for no special privileges because of his special skill, ability, or desires, but will joyfully place himself on the same level with his fellows and accept the common lot. When a man receives according to his need, he is doing unto others as he would have them do unto him. Here again, this principle of distribution is taken for granted in the human family, and we feel that it should be also in the spiritual family.

A third family principle is that there must be no favorite children, whether they are blondes or brunettes, white or black. When the Bible says that God is no respecter of persons, it is simply stating that God has no favorite children, that he has created no superior race, that fellowship with him is a matter of the heart and not of the skin, and that every individual has equal access to the Father's love and to that of the rest of the brethren. In his church community, God will allow no partition walls which divide men into race, caste, or nation. We at Koinonia wish to worship God neither in Jerusalem nor Samaria, neither at the shrine of our ancestors nor of Southern traditions, but in spirit and in truth. We joyfully accept as a brother anyone whom the Father begets as a son.

A fourth principle of the Koinonia is that the sons of the Father will increasingly become partakers of his nature, which is redemptive love. He is not a God of violence, hate, and revenge. His method of destroying his enemies is to transform them into his sons. He woos them with an everlasting love, until they make a voluntary response of love to his love. He never overcomes his enemies by frightening them by force or coercion. He is a God of peace, of steadfast love, of unfailing good will. To us at Koinonia this means a renunciation of all warfare and violence and a dedication of ourselves to love, peace, and good will. We do not participate in the armed services. Though we as a group have been attacked with dynamite and gunshot, we have not responded with such. We earnestly desire an increasing measure of the Father's nature which will enable us to love our enemies and do good to those who despitefully use us.

from *The Cotton Patch Version of Luke and Acts* (1969)[21]

"Jesus' Doings", Luke, Chapter 4.

Verse 14. Jesus, spiritually invigorated, returned to south Georgia, and the news of him spread through the whole area. He was speaking in their churches, and the people respected him. But he went to Valdosta, where he had grown up, and as he was in the habit of doing, he went to church on Sunday. They invited him to preach, so he got up to read the scripture and found the place in the book of Isaiah where it says:

"The Lord's spirit is on me;
He has ordained me to break the good news to the poor people.
He has sent me to proclaim freedom for the oppressed,
And sight for the blind,
To help those who have been grievously insulted to find dignity;
To proclaim the Lord's new era."

Verse 20. Then he closed the Bible, and handed it to the assistant minister. The eyes of everybody in the congregation were glued on him. He began by saying, "This very day this Scripture has become a reality in your presence." They all said, "Amen," and were amazed at the eloquent words flowing from his mouth. They whispered to one another, "Can this really be old Joe's boy?"

"Happenings", Acts, Chapter 2.

Verse 42. They were all bound together . . . by the sense of community, by the common meal and the prayers. . . . The whole company of believers stuck together and held all things common. They were selling their goods and belongings, and dividing them among the group on the basis of one's need. Knit together with singleness of purpose they gathered at the church every day, and as they ate the common meal from house to house they had a joyful and humble spirit, praising God and showing over-flowing kindness toward everybody. And day by day, as people were being rescued, the Lord would add them to the fellowship.

Chapter 4. Verse 32. Now a single heart and soul was in the body of believers. Not one of them considered his property to be private, but all things were shared by them. With mighty power the apostles were giving the evidence of Jesus' aliveness, and upon them all was a spirit of abounding goodwill. You know, there wasn't a person in the group in need. For owners of land or houses were selling them and bringing the proceeds and placing them at the disposal of the apostles. Distribution was then made to everyone on the basis of his need.

from *The Cotton Patch Version of Paul's Epistles* (1968)[22]

"The Letter to the Churches of the Georgia Convention" Galatians, Chapter 5.

Verse 14. [S]erve one another in a spirit of love. For the whole social code can be summed up in one sentence: Love your neighbor as yourself. . . .

Verse 16. My advice is: Walk in the Spirit, and don't let human desire go to seed. For the body has it in for the conscience, and the conscience has it in for the body, for the two are directly opposed to each other. That is why you cannot run wild, doing as you please. Now if you are guided by the conscience, you are not under the sway of social custom. . . .

Verse 22. . . . [T]he results of the Spirit-led life are love, joy, peace, patience, kindness, goodness, loyalty, humility and self-control.

"The Letter to the Christians in Birmingham" Ephesians, Chapter 2.

Verse 11. . . . [A]lways remember that previously you Negroes . . . were at one time outside the Christian fellowship, denied your rights as fellow believers, and treated as though the gospel didn't apply to you, hopeless and God-forsaken in the eyes of the world. Now, however, because of Christ's supreme sacrifice, you who once were so segregated are warmly welcomed into the Christian fellowship.

[Verse] 14. He himself is our peace. It was he who integrated us and abolished the segregation patterns which caused so much hostility. He

allowed no silly traditions and customs in his fellowship, so that in it he might integrate the two into one new body. In this way he healed the hurt, and by his sacrifice on the cross he joined together both sides into one body for God. In it the hostility no longer exists.

Verse 17. When he came, he preached the same message of peace to those on both the inside and outside. In him we both found a common spiritual approach to the Father. So then, you are no longer segregated and pushed around, but you are fellow citizens with all Christians and respected members of God's family. This is based on the unshakable foundation Jesus himself laid down through the apostles and other men of God, with Christ being the cornerstone. Around him all the rest of the building is fitted together into a dedicated temple of the Lord. And you all are a vital part of God's spiritual dwelling place.

NOTES

1. Information on the life of Clarence Jordan can be found in Dallas Lee, *The Cotton Patch Evidence* (New York: Harper & Row, 1971); James William McClendon Jr., *Biography as Theology: How Life Stories Can Remake Today's Theology* (Nashville: Abingdon Press, 1974); Millard Fuller, *Bokotola* (New York: Association Press, 1977); and P. Joel Snider, *The "Cotton Patch" Gospel: The Proclamation of Clarence Jordan* (Lanham, Md.: University Press of America, 1985).

2. Lee, *The Cotton Patch Evidence*, 10.

3. Ibid., 22.

4. Cited in Snider, *The "Cotton Patch" Gospel*, 93.

5. Ibid., 48.

6. Lee, *The Cotton Patch Evidence*, 76.

7. Snider, *The "Cotton Patch" Gospel*, 35.

8. Clarence Jordan, "The Meaning of Christian Fellowship," *Prophetic Religion* 7 (1946): 4.

9. Clarence Jordan, *The Cotton Patch Version of Luke and Acts: Jesus' Doings and the Happenings* (Piscataway, N.J.: New Century Publishers, 1969), 95.

10. Charles Nordhoff, *The Communistic Societies of the United States* (New York: Harper & Brothers, 1875).

11. Robert S. Fogarty, *American Utopianism* (Itasca, Ill.: F.E. Peacock Publishers, 1972); Lee, *The Cotton Patch Evidence*, 93–104.

12. H. Shelton Smith, *In His Image, But . . . : Racism in Southern Religion* (Durham, N.C.: Duke University Press, 1972), 305; John Lee Eighmy, *Churches in Cultural Captivity: A History of the Social Attitudes of Southern Baptists* (Knoxville: University of Tennessee Press, 1972); Samuel S. Hill Jr. *Southern Churches in Crisis* (New York: Holt, Rinehart & Winston, 1966).

13. Gibson Winter, *The Suburban Captivity of the Churches: An Analysis of Protestant Responsibility in the Expanding Metropolis* (New York: Doubleday, 1961).

14. Eventually the farm grew to fourteen hundred acres. "Clarence Jordan," *The Christian Century* 86 (12 November 1969): 1442.

15. Jordan, *The Cotton Patch Version of Luke and Acts*, 100.

16. Clarence Jordan, *The Cotton Patch Version of Paul's Epistles*, (New York: Association Press, 1968), 106–8.

17. "Clarence Jordan," *Christian Century* 86 (12 November 1969): 1442; "Koinonia Updated," *Christian Century* 93 (13 October 1976): 868.

18. "Koinonia Updated," *Christian Century* 93 (13 October 1976): 869; Charles W. Blaker, "The Koinonia Community: Not by Might, Nor by Power," *Christianity and Crisis* 40 (24 November 1980): 331–33.

19. Jimmy Carter, *Living Faith* (New York: Times Books, 1996).

20. Clarence Jordan, "Christian Community in the South," *The Journal of Religious Thought* 14, no. 1 (autumn-winter 1956–1957): 27–30. Used by permission.

21. Jordan, *The Cotton Patch Version of Luke and Acts: Jesus' Doings and the Happenings*, 24, 95–96, 100. Permission by New Win Publishing, Clinton, N.J..

22. Jordan, *The Cotton Patch Version of Paul's Epistles*, 102, 106–8. Permission by New Win Publishing, Clinton, N.J..

8.

ORLANDO E. COSTAS
(1942–1987)

Theologian and Missiologist:
Enlarging the Scope of Christian Conversion

n the 1950s—and for a generation thereafter—a number of evangelicals
sought to widen the narrow conception of Christian conversion that
had been common among their fundamentalist predecessors. C. S.
Lewis, the literary sage of theologically conservative Protestants, captured
the post-World War II "neo-evangelical" outlook in his popular *Chronicles
of Narnia*. In this 1951 fantasy, Lewis described a scene in which, after several years' absence, a young girl named Lucy meets up with Aslan, a Christ-
figured talking lion.

> She gazed up into the large wise face.
> "Welcome, child," he said.
> "Aslan," said Lucy, "you're bigger."
> "That is because you are older, little one," answered he.
> "Not because you are?"
> "I am not. But every year you grow, you will find me bigger."[1]

A short time after the publication of Lewis's story, Orlando Costas, a
seventeen-year-old, Puerto Rican immigrant to the United States, was converted to Christ at Billy Graham's 1957 New York Crusade. That spiritual
event became the foundation for Costas's entire ministry. But in subsequent years, drawing from his life experience as a Hispanic American,
Costas's understanding of the scope of Christian conversion underwent a
dramatic transformation. Like Lewis's character, Lucy, Costas's perception
of God and God's work enlarged as he grew in his knowledge of himself
and others. Conversion to Christ led Costas to experience a conversion to
his culture and, eventually, a conversion to the world, "especially the world
of the forgotten and exploited."[2]

Coping With
"A Strange Environment"

Orlando E. Costas was born into a middle-class Methodist family in Puerto Rico. His mother consecrated him to God's service even before his birth. In 1954, when Costas was twelve, his father's grocery business failed. Few economic options were available on the island, so his family decided to move to the continental United States, a pattern followed by many other Puerto Ricans during this period.

Puerto Rico has had a troubled history in relation to the United States. Ceded to the United States by Spain as a result of the Spanish-American War, Puerto Rico is, in Costas's words, "one of the last overt colonies in the hemisphere." Technically, Puerto Rico is a commonwealth, which means that Puerto Ricans are U.S. citizens but have no voting representation in Congress. Over the years, American business people have tended to view Puerto Rico callously as a source of cheap labor, while Puerto Ricans have viewed the United States with a mixture of suspicion, resentment, and longing—longing for the material prosperity of the mainland.[3]

In the 1950s, two and one-half million people lived on the island, with a population density of nearly seven hundred inhabitants per square mile. In those years very few industries had been established, so the mostly agrarian populace eked out its living on small, soil-depleted farms or as ill-treated workers on huge sugar plantations. Faced with ever-deepening poverty, many Puerto Ricans sought employment in the urban centers of the U.S. mainland. The migrant subculture that developed among Puerto Ricans in the United States was split in two directions: older immigrants continued to channel their cultural allegiance back toward Puerto Rico while their children were drawn toward the consumerism flaunted by the dominant Anglo-American culture.[4]

Protestant Puerto Rican immigrants, such as the Costas family, were in a particularly difficult position culturally. When they lived in the overwhelmingly Roman Catholic milieu of Puerto Rico, Protestants found support for their minority religious status from U.S. missionaries. When these Puerto Rican Protestants immigrated to the United States, they expected to feel connected to mainstream American Protestant culture.[5] The Costas family, for example, became part of the Hispanic Evangelical Mission in Bridgeport, Connecticut, sponsored by the local Protestant Council of Churches. The mission church was a sort of social refuge for Orlando Costas and his siblings.

Outside of the church, however, Costas was treated just as poorly as other Puerto Ricans. He had come to the States with a boyish, middle-class confidence, but that changed when he encountered the reality of Hispanic North America—"a strange environment, full of hostility and prejudice."

He was ridiculed simply because of his ethnicity. His father was unable to obtain a decent job. This oppressive situation produced "a profound and traumatic culture shock" within Costas. He resented the run-down, unheated apartment in which they lived. He developed feelings of shame and self-hatred that he acted out through aggressive social behavior. And he rebelled against his family and their expression of Christianity—mocking his mother's faith, ignoring his father's discipline, and bullying his sisters. By his own account, he was hotheaded and egocentric.[6]

At the invitation of a group of friends, Costas attended Billy Graham's evangelistic crusade in New York. He had been "trying to push God out" of his life, but God was not so easily pushed. In response to the evangelist's invitation to "come forward," he made a public profession of faith by walking to the front of the auditorium—a "quasi sacramental . . . outward means" through which he expressed his commitment to Christ. Costas looked upon this experience as the beginning of his spiritual journey. As he stated: "something unique . . . happen[ed] on June 8, 1957 in Madison Square Garden, and has been happening ever since."[7]

The venue for Costas's conversion was significant. Billy Graham (born 1918) was the symbolic leader of Protestant evangelicalism in the second half of the twentieth century, the heir to the revivalistic tradition of Charles Finney, D. L. Moody, J. Wilbur Chapman, and Billy Sunday. Like them, Graham emphasized the normativeness of a "born again" conversion experience. Educated at Bob Jones University and Wheaton College, Graham had strong fundamentalist credentials, but he tailored his evangelistic style to fit the less-rigid religiosity of post-World War II America.[8]

Though unbeknown to Costas, Graham's 1957 New York crusade was something of a watershed event within conservative Protestant circles. At that crusade, Graham asked Martin Luther King Jr. to join him on the platform to lead the crusade in prayer. This action incurred the wrath of many whites in the South, causing Graham to receive death threats and to be vilified publicly as a "communist." Also at the New York crusade, Graham began his practice of accepting the backing of any Christian pastor who was interested in supporting his evangelistic efforts—including mainline, ecumenically oriented Protestant leaders.[9]

Graham's "cooperative evangelism" and his rejection of racial bigotry were both indicative of the religious perspective of the postwar generation of evangelicals. These "new," or "neo-," evangelicals desired to maintain their commitment to a Biblically oriented personal gospel, but they disagreed with the inflexibility of the older fundamentalism. The neo-evangelical overtures to a broader Christianity resulted in bitter opposition from the fundamentalists, especially from Graham's former mentor, Bob Jones (1883–1968), who considered Graham to be a compromiser of the faith, since he entertained a "soft" attitude toward liberals.[10]

Given Costas's spiritual indebtedness to Graham's relatively open style of evangelism, it is ironic that Costas, through the recommendation of his local pastor, ended up attending the college preparatory program at Bob Jones University in Greenville, South Carolina. There, Costas was subjected to North American fundamentalism in its most severe form. The theological conservatism of the school did not perturb Costas as much as its social conservatism. He was deeply bothered and offended by the exaltation of Anglo-Saxon culture, the uncontested justification of racism, and the school's triumphalistic promotion of their belief in the manifest destiny of the United States. Nevertheless, similar to the experiences of Charles Stelzle, E. Stanley Jones, and Clarence Jordan, all of whom attended conservative schools, Costas was able to appropriate some important learnings from his time at Bob Jones University. For instance, it was there that he discovered the Christian imperative for evangelism and mission, which became the central focus of his subsequent ministry. Even more significantly, through his interaction with other Latin American students at the school, Costas rediscovered his previously hidden Hispanic identity. He became aware of the particularity of his own culture in spite of its virtual exclusion from most expressions of conservative Anglo-American religion.

Costas realized that the biracial construction of social reality he experienced at Bob Jones—in which Southern culture was divided into sharply defined white and black worlds—did not make any room for his ethnic identity. Such a binary worldview did not allow for a multicultural view of reality, which was (and is) most descriptive of the ethnic diversity of U.S. society. Consequently, as Costas pursued his education amid the largely Anglo world of conservative Protestantism, he had to find his own way culturally. At Bob Jones, and later at Nyack Missionary College, Winona Lake School of Theology, and Trinity Evangelical Divinity School, Costas stayed in touch with the Hispanic community through evangelism and preaching. He also served several part-time Baptist and Disciples of Christ pastorates in storefront Hispanic congregations. And although he took the time to attend Garrett Evangelical Seminary and to obtain a doctorate in Missiology from the Free University of Amsterdam, his most cherished educational experience was his study of Latin American history and culture at the University of Puerto Rico.

It was through all of these events that Costas overcame his personal "cultural crisis" and experienced "an authentic cultural conversion"—which he viewed as an outgrowth of his earlier conversion to Christ. Indeed, Costas was convinced that it was his initial encounter with Jesus as Savior and Lord that had opened him up to be able to interact meaningfully with the people of his own culture. While maintaining his evangelical spirituality, he consciously broke away from the Anglo-American orientation of his Protestant upbringing and academic formation, a process that Latino theologian Paulo Freire has called "conscientization."[11]

Conversion to the World

During his pastorate in Milwaukee, Costas came to realize that the Hispanic immigrants with whom he ministered lacked a sustained political organization that would advocate for their concerns. Consequently, Costas became involved in community organizing, specifically in the establishment of the Latin American Union for Civil Rights. As he struggled to empower Latinos politically, Costas's conscience was raised regarding the need for the church to practice its mission comprehensively. He was led to "discover the world of the poor and the disenfranchised as a fundamental reference of the Gospel." Costas began to see that a "total missionary practice" for the church would include an emphasis on the social, economic, and political needs of people as well as the traditional Protestant focus on evangelism and the importance of personal faith in Christ.[12]

Costas's conversion to the world was the fruit of his pastoral experience among the poor of Milwaukee. This action-reflection concept of ministry among marginalized people was indicative of the influence of liberation theology on some North American Christians from the late 1960s through the 1980s. Liberation theology developed originally in Latin America among activist Roman Catholic priests in the years following the second Vatican Council. More particularly, liberationist thought gained momentum during the Latin American Bishops Conference held in Medellín, Colombia, in 1968. According to its leading spokesman, Peruvian priest Gustavo Gutiérrez (born 1928), the theology of liberation begins with one's Christian praxis on behalf of the disenfranchised of society and then moves to theological reflection based on that concrete action. This basic commitment to work among marginalized people results from the conviction of liberation theologians that God provides affluent Christians with an opportunity to stand in solidarity with God's "preferential option for the poor." (Interestingly, the liberationist sense of solidarity with the poor is similar to the earlier views of Vida Scudder and Clarence Jordan.) In the words of Gutiérrez, to opt in favor of the poor is to opt "for the God of the kingdom" as proclaimed and lived by Jesus.[13]

Costas and other North Americans who adopted insights from liberation theology determined that the church was obligated to minister to the "world in its complexity and concreteness." When applied to the specific social situation of the United States, this service-oriented mission of the church had a particular focus toward the "poor" of North American society—a term intended to be representative of all oppressed persons, including Hispanic Americans, African Americans, Native Americans, women, and others. Marginalized people were encouraged to take responsibility for their own liberation. Meanwhile, the privileged Christians of North American society were called on to work in conjunction with the poor for the achievement of the full humanization of men and women.[14]

A Dynamic, Dialectical
Understanding of Conversion

Costas grafted his appropriation of certain aspects of liberation theology onto his evangelical understanding of conversion and Christian devotion. As a result, his evangelicalism broadened so that he no longer viewed conversion as a "static, . . . non-contextual event" but rather as a "dynamic, complex experience." He redefined conversion as "a plunge into an ongoing adventure . . . a journey into the mystery of the kingdom of God, which leads from one experience to another." Costas's characterization of conversion as a continuous "adventure" is similar to the interpretations of Christian spirituality put forward by Vida Scudder, E. Stanley Jones and, more recently, by Gustavo Gutiérrez.[15]

Costas first experienced conversion as a distinct moment of repentance toward God. Later, he experienced conversion as a recurrent process of repentance—successive "new turning points" that moved him away from sin (and selfishness) and toward God (and God's work in the world). Costas never lost a sense of the importance and essentiality of his initial spiritual transformation in Christ, which he considered to be the "fundamental point of reference" for his life. Nonetheless, he did not consider this fundamental religious reference point to be a fixed spiritual location. Rather, Costas understood his evangelical conversion to be a "foundational signpost that accompanies one along throughout the journey, similar to the traveling tabernacle in the Old Testament"—an image many people have found helpful as they try to live out a holistic Gospel that combines piety and justice.[16]

Costas also believed that the enabling power of the Holy Spirit draws those who are being converted into connection with the Kingdom of God. This identification means that Christians will have a dialectical relationship with the surrounding culture. On the one hand, the values of the society will become less important as God's values become preeminent. On the other hand, the needs of the broader society become the "top priority in their Christian vocation." Costas felt that believers were to be *for* the world, but not *of* the world.[17]

Like many of the other nineteenth-and twentieth-century persons we have studied, Costas's emphasis on the Kingdom of God led him to perceive the systemic nature of structural sins—especially in the church. He noted that "not only individual believers, but the church as a whole in a given geographical area can be trapped into sin." The call to conversion is therefore extended to the entire U.S. church, which itself "has to be liberated in order to be a liberating agent in the world."[18]

In the United States, this missional task will not be addressed in the same way that it would be elsewhere, for different situational contexts demand different forms of response to the claims of the gospel. Costas articulated the concept of a "contextual evangelism," in which the call to conversion is presented in a culturally specific form that will both enrich and critically evaluate each particular social milieu.[19]

Costas and Other
Progressive Evangelicals

Orlando Costas represented a group of so-called "young evangelicals" during the 1970s who promoted a ministry of evangelism and social justice. Just as William Goodell and other nineteenth-century abolitionists built upon—but then went beyond—Charles Finney's rather cautious interest in social involvement, so Costas and his young evangelical allies inherited the initial social stirrings of Billy Graham and the neo-evangelicals, but then went further. The efforts of the progressive young evangelicals included the establishment of a number of activistic journals, such as *Sojourners, Prism, Daughters of Sarah, The Other Side, Radix,* and *Transformation,* and the development of sociopolitical advocacy groups like Evangelicals for Social Action, the Seamless Garment Network, and, in the 1990s, the Call to Renewal. These organizations hoped to influence social legislation from a faith-based perspective.[20]

In 1987, not long after he became Dean at Andover-Newton Theological School, Costas's untimely death due to stomach cancer left progressive evangelicalism bereft of one of its foremost theological voices. However, in combination with the work of earlier leaders, a new generation of committed Christians picked up the challenge of contextual evangelism and social change. In the 1980s and 1990s, several new church-based intentional communities arose (somewhat similar to Clarence Jordan's Koinonia Farm), such as Jubilee Partners in Georgia, the Church of the Redeemer in Houston, and Azusa Christian Community in Boston—which was modeled directly after William Seymour's interracial mission in Los Angeles. In addition, an informal network of authors, editors, pastors, lecturers, and political activists resulted in a phalanx of evangelistic social action enterprises. Like Costas, these progressive evangelical ministries sought to enlarge the arena of Christian conversion to include both a personal commitment to Christ and a social commitment to the world.[21]

Selections From the
Writings of Orlando E. Costas

from "Conversion as a Complex Experience: A Hispanic Case Study," (1978)[22]

This paper is an exploration of the Christian understanding of conversion as a dynamic, complex experience. . . . I use, first, a *concentric* model to explain the facts related to my "complex conversion experience." I thus speak of a religious conversion to Christ, a cultural conversion to Puerto Rico and Latin America, and a sociopolitical (or missional) conversion to the world, particularly the world of the poor and disenfranchised of society. I do not see these conversion experiences as divorced from one another, but as interrelated. Thus the conversion to Christ is foundational, the cultural a consequence of my new identity in Christ, and the sociopolitical an outgrowth of my calling as a follower of the man who wants to be found among the destitute of the earth. My encounter with an African friend showed me, however, that even this way of formulating the complexity of my conversion experience was too static. I suggest, accordingly, a second model, namely, that of a *spiral*, as a more adequate way of understanding the meaning of conversion. . . .

A Concentric Model of Conversion

Allow me to describe [my] pilgrimage in three concentric circles. The center is Christ, of course, and the first circle represents my conversion to Him.

Conversion to Christ. [While I was at a Billy Graham crusade, . . .] the words of the hymn the choir was singing at the moment of the invitation had a moving impact on me. "Just as I am without one plea but that thy blood was shed for me". . . . I decided to respond affirmatively to the invitation that was being extended by the Evangelist and *made the words of the hymn my own.*

The quasi sacramental act of going forward and the personal prayer of confession I made later became the outward means through which I expressed my commitment to Christ. The evidence that something positive and unusual had occurred was the change of attitude I began to demonstrate several hours later. When I arrived home that evening, the first thing I did was tell my mother that I had been converted to Jesus Christ and that I had begun a new life. . . .

Conversion to Culture. . . . [I began] to question the political hegemony of the USA in Latin America and to consciously break with its culture.

This did not mean that I had become hostile to North Americans as persons. It meant rather that I was becoming increasingly aware of the political oppression and economic exploitation which their nation, as an imperial and neo-colonial power, was exercising over Latin America as a whole, and in particular, over my own country. It meant, further, that I had finally come face to face with the fact that I was not an Anglo-American; that I needed not to be one for I had a rich cultural heritage of my own which I should accept joyfully; and, therefore, that I should aim at getting rid of any Anglo-American cultural influence which stood in the way of the full expression of my Puerto Rican and Latin American cultural heritage.

I had overcome my cultural crisis. I had experienced an authentic cultural conversion, an experience which was not isolated from other moments in my life. For in a sense, it was the outgrowth of the tensions I had lived from my first contacts with Anglo-Saxon culture. And in a deeper sense, it had been stimulated and inspired by my encounter with that Jew who had transformed my existence once I acknowledged Him as God's revelation made flesh and trusted Him as my only Savior and Lord.

Conversion to the world. . . . I got involved in community organization, helping to organize the Latin American Union for Civil Rights.

I should say that in this political praxis I never lost my Christian and pastoral identity. On the contrary, this process led me to reflect critically on my ministry and on the nature and mission of the church. This led me to discover the world of the poor and the disenfranchised as a fundamental reference of the Gospel. I came to realize that the Christian mission had not only personal, spiritual and cultural dimensions, but also social, economic and political. This meant that the object of mission was not the community of faith, but the world in its complexity and concreteness. . . .

My conversions to Christ and to my culture had been complemented by a conversion to the world, *especially the world of the forgotten and exploited*. . . .

A Spiral Model of Conversion

. . . While visiting Cameroon, I had the occasion to share my three-fold conversion experiences with an African friend and theologian. . . . He answered: "So you think those will be your only conversions? If they are, then their validity will have been denied. For if you are to continue to grow as a person and as a Christian, you will have to experience one turn after another."

Those words made me think . . . and to change my concentric model into a *spiral* one. For the complexity of conversion does not lie in a fixed number of experiences, but in the fact that it is a plunge into an ongoing adventure. Christian conversion is a journey into the mystery of the kingdom of God, which leads from one experience to another.

From this definition, it follows that while Christian conversion can be signified by a distinct moment, it is also an ongoing process. Initiation in the journey of the kingdom implies a plunge into an eschatological adventure where one is confronted with ever new decisions, ever new turning points, ever new fulfillments and ever new promises, and this will continue until the ultimate fulfillment of the kingdom. It also implies that one is confronted with the need to make ever new re-turnings to the fundamental point of reference and engage in ever new re-routings. The fundamental point of reference, however, is not a static, fixed point, but a foundational signpost that accompanies one along throughout the journey, similar to the traveling tabernacle in the Old Testament or the *anamnesis* [remembrance] that the children of Israel engaged in year after year in the Passover celebration: a celebration and living again, at whatever point of their pilgrimage, [of] the Passover experience. . . .

Conversion, . . . which has a distinct, though not a consciously uniform beginning, implies a constant turning from the self to God. Obsession with the self alienates women and men from their human vocation, from their calling in creation to be at the service of one another. The self is the idol which separates them not only from their vocation, but from their creator. In turning to God, they are reconciled to the true source of life and are renewed in their vocation. Conversion is, therefore, a passage from a dehumanized and de-humanizing existence to a humanized and humanizing life. . . .

We should [also] think of conversion as a socio-ecclesial reality. Social, because it is historical. It is not something which occurs in a vacuum. It takes place in particular social contexts. These contexts bear witness and are witnessed to by conversion. . . .

Conversion constitutes a break with and a new commitment to society. It places believers in a dialectical relation with their environment. Society becomes penultimate in their scale of values. At the same time, society becomes top priority in their Christian vocation. Free from its absorbing power, believers can give themselves completely to the service of their respective societies. . . .

Conversion is an ecclesial reality. It is the result of the witnessing engagement of a visible, concrete community, and leads to incorporation into that community. This implies a new set of relationships, participation in a new fellowship, witnessing with others to a new social reality and sharing in the hope of a new future. . . . This community, however, is affected by the tensions of history. It is constantly threatened by what the New Testament calls the principalities and powers of evil. . . . Not only individual believers, but the church as a whole in a given geographical area can be trapped into sin. . . . [T]he call to conversion is not limited to unbelievers and individual believers who have fallen into sin, but is extended to the church. . . . [M]ission is always a two-way street, a going-coming, outer-inner reality. The church can only be *inside-out,* if it is *outside-in.* In order to minister, it must be ministered to; in order to call others to conversion, [the church] must be converted itself. We have seen how sin and evil are a constant threat to the church. Whenever the church falls into this trap, it enters into a situation of (functional) disbelief, its life and mission become corrupted, it becomes deaf to God's word and loses touch with the Holy Spirit. In such occasions, the call to conversion inside the church becomes a missional priority. . . .

In all of this, we should not forget that though the church might be unfaithful, God remains faithful, and that though conversion involves our human responsibility, it is made possible because of the sovereignty of God's grace. "Turning" and "returning" are thus gifts which God invites us to accept in Jesus Christ and enables us to appropriate by the liberating action of his Spirit. . . .

While not everyone experiences conversion in the same way, nevertheless, there is ample evidence in Scripture and in Christian theology to substantiate the idea of a[n] . . . open-ended process, grounded on a vital, initial encounter with and acceptance of Christ as Savior and Lord. This fact becomes thereafter a key that enables believers to unlock the many turning points in the course of their spiritual pilgrimage. Thus, for example, my cultural conversion is not an isolated, secular experience, but one which finds its roots in Christ. My conversion to Christ is a fundamental reference in my interpretation and evaluation of other conversions which I may have in my pilgrimage.

NOTES

1. C. S. Lewis, *Prince Caspian: The Return to Narnia* (New York: Collier Books, 1970; original publication, 1951), 136.

2. Orlando E. Costas, "Conversion as a Complex Experience: A Hispanic Case Study," *Occasional Essays* 5 (June 1978): 30.

3. Costas, "Conversion as a Complex Experience," 22; Eldin Villafañe, *The Liberating Spirit: Toward an Hispanic American Pentecostal Social Ethic* (Grand Rapids, Mich.: Wm. B. Eerdmans Publishing Co., 1993), 37–38.

4. Villafañe, *The Liberating Spirit*, 39.

5. See Guillermo Cook, *The Expectation of the Poor: Latin American Basic Ecclesial Communities in Protestant Perspective* (Maryknoll, N.Y.: Orbis Books, 1985), 200–05, 221–22, 230–31.

6. Costas, "Conversion as a Complex Experience," 24.

7. Ibid., 25–26.

8. George M. Marsden, *Understanding Fundamentalism and Evangelicalism* (Grand Rapids, Mich.: Wm. B. Eerdmans Publishing Co., 1991), 67–71.

9. Ibid., 73.

10. Ibid., 71–73.

11. Costas, "Conversion as a Complex Experience," 29; Paulo Freire, *Pedagogy for the Oppressed* (New York: Herder & Herder, 1970).

12. Costas, "Conversion as a Complex Experience," 30.

13. Gustavo Gutiérrez, *A Theology of Liberation* (Maryknoll, N.Y.: Orbis Books, 1988; original ed., 1971), xvii–xxxiv.

14. Costas, "Conversion as a Complex Experience," 30, 34.

15. Ibid., 21, 31; Gustavo Gutiérrez, *We Drink From Our Own Wells: The Spiritual Journey of a People* (Maryknoll, N.Y.: Orbis Books, 1984), 88–89.

16. Costas, "Conversion as a Complex Experience," 31–33.

17. Ibid., 35.

18. Ibid., 36–40.

19. Orlando E. Costas, *Liberating News: A Theology of Contextual Evangelization* (Grand Rapids, Mich: Wm. B. Eerdmans Publishing Co., 1989).

20. Richard Quebedeaux, *The Young Evangelicals: Revolution in Orthodoxy* (New York: Harper & Row, 1974) and *The Worldly Evangelicals* (New York: Harper & Row, 1978).

21. See Eldin Villafañe, "An Evangelical Call to a Social Spirituality," in Arturo J. Bañuelas, ed., *Mestizo Christianity: Theology from the Latino Perspective* (Maryknoll, N.Y.: Orbis Books, 1995).

22. Costas, "Conversion as a Complex Experience: A Hispanic Case Study," *Occasional Essays* 5 (June 1978): 21–40; reprinted in Robert T. Coote and John R.W. Stott, eds., *Down to Earth: Studies in Christianity and Culture, The Papers of the Lausanne Consultation on Gospel and Culture* (Grand Rapids: Wm. B. Eerdmans Co. 1980). Used by permission of the U.S. Lausanne Committee.

CONCLUSION

Protestant spirituality has relied heavily on the theological testimony of the apostle Paul—particularly the way in which his message was formulated in the epistle to the Galatians.[1] In that letter, Paul placed a great deal of emphasis on the tenet that men and women enter into a right relationship to God by faith in Jesus Christ, not by depending on their good works (see especially Gal. 2:16). Paul also argued that the motivation to love our neighbors cannot be manufactured by the effort of our will or imposed by external religious authority. Instead, self-giving love will issue forth from the wellspring of a regenerated heart, the transformation of the human spirit by the Holy Spirit. Paul was persuaded that the only dependable religious basis for acting righteously on behalf of others was a disciplined life that was lived in the power of the Spirit. Thereby, he sought to provide a firm spiritual foundation for Christian activism.

By emphasizing an individual's trust in God, Paul did not intend for Christians to prioritize personal religiosity over virtuous action; indeed, there was to be no functional separation of works from faith. Neither should Paul's perception of the new creation in Christ ever be interpreted as other-worldly or privatistic, for God's spiritual renewal of human beings is always brought about in the context of the communal body of Christ. The regeneration of character and the regeneration of society go hand-in-hand.

Clarence Jordan's translation of Galatians contemporized Paul's message of inward renewal and outward action. Jordan described the practice of Christianity as a "Spirit-led life" of participation in "the God movement"—his term for the Kingdom of God. The God movement comes about whenever people "serve one another in a spirit of love." The formation of our souls by the Spirit of God leads to the transformation of society by the spirit of human love. Given this basic understanding of God's purpose for humanity, Paul's (and Jordan's) advice to the church was unmistakable: the people of God are called to "walk in the Spirit" (Gal. 5:13–16).[2]

The women and men portrayed in this book walked in the Spirit according to Paul's holistic understanding. For example, when William Goodell appropriated Finney's revivalistic fervor, he applied it to the radical reorganization of political, social, and ecclesiastical structures. Julia Foote drew from the deep resources of her spiritual rebirth and sanctification to challenge the entrenched gender and racial discrimination of the late nineteenth century. Fueled by the power of Holy Spirit baptism, William Seymour envisioned and actually initiated a multicultural community—during one of the most racist periods in U.S. history. And, inwardly enlivened by his born-again experience, Orlando Costas expanded the conceptualization of conversion to encompass the liberation of marginalized people everywhere.

Common Marks of the Spirit-led Life

At the conclusion of our exploration into the lives of these eight who walked in the Spirit, it is appropriate to determine what, if any, characteristics they held in common. Despite the particularity of each person's historical and cultural context, the men and women in this anthology shared three basic attributes: a regenerative faith experience, a vision of human interrelatedness, and a critique of conventional religious and social structures.

First, and fundamentally, the persons represented in this book had a deeply personal, even intimate relationship with God, based on an experience of spiritual regeneration in Christ. Although the topic of spirituality is currently quite popular, the discussion is often vague—sometimes without any articulation of specific religious content. The individuals depicted here would have allowed no such imprecision. They were all theologians, whether formally or informally, who thoughtfully reflected on their religious experience. As we have seen, none of these people pictured their spirituality in a mystical way that could not be described concretely. They were determined to bring their knowledge of God down to earth. In fact, they provided substantive, articulate analyses of their theological views expressly because they believed that their spirituality was a gift to be shared with others.

Consequently, we have been able to ascertain the content of the religious commitment and to get at the heart of the spirituality of all of the persons portrayed in this anthology. While they differed in their particular theological expression, in each case we have seen that their faith was affective and conversionistic. That is, they all promoted, in the words of E. Stanley Jones, a "first-hand contagious experience of the living Christ."[3] Orlando Costas described his conversion similarly, as an "open-ended process, grounded on a vital, initial encounter with and acceptance of Christ as Savior and Lord."[4] These were serious-minded Christians who had a deep yearning for God's presence. Their spiritual experiences were Biblically grounded and Christ-centered. In short, they manifested a piety that, according to standard interpretations of American religious history, should be understood as "evangelical."

Having said that, however, the type of evangelicalism practiced by those who walked in the Spirit—what we might call a progressive evangelicalism—must be immediately distinguished from that represented generally by popular American piety. The typical religion of evangelical Protestants in the United States has often become so internalized that it has been reduced to little more than spiritual narcissism. Some present-day expressions of faith, for instance, are concerned only with sustaining an intense level of religious experience. In such cases, the enhancement of the experience itself becomes all-important (the focus of spirituality thereby placed on our feelings), rather than viewing convictional experiences in the New Testament sense as a consequential manifestation of Christ's regeneration (in which the focus of spirituality is placed on Christ's work in us for the sake of the world). Orlando Costas recognized this tendency within Protestant spirituality and, in response, stated that the goal of conversion is "not to provide a series of emotional trips" but, rather, to put believers "at the service of the mission of God's kingdom."[5]

The men and women in this book trusted in the salvific work that Jesus had done for them on the cross and then tried to live in faithful response to that assurance of pardon in order to be in ministry to others. Clarence Jordan, for example, was not interested in experiencing more of God's grace for his own benefit. Rather, he was interested in "how much grace I can receive that I may be able to give help; how strong I can get in grace that I may be able to help the poor person who is really thirsting and hungering for grace."[6]

Another difficulty with certain expressions of current spirituality is related to U.S. society's overemphasis on individual autonomy. In our Enlightenment-influenced American culture, personal identities have become primary while community-building is optional. In such a culture, it is easy for the spiritual life to develop unhealthy elements of interiority and hyperindividualism. A person's relationship to God is seen as a solitary transaction between "Jesus and me"—the lone, pious individual striving to be Christlike. In the words of a well-loved, early twentieth-century hymn:

I come to the garden alone, while the dew is still on the roses,
   And the voice I hear, falling on my ear, the Son of God discloses.
   And He walks with me and He talks with me, and He tells me I
am His own,
   And the joy we share as we tarry there, none other has ever
known.[7]

With such a privatistic piety, social questions—if addressed at all—merely become derivative of one's personal decision for Christ. Faith becomes disconnected from the larger body of Christ, and (except for evangelism and philanthropy) from the problems of society. The "spiritual" life has been redefined as a relationship with God standing apart from the temporal concerns of human existence. As the Statement of Faith of a conservative seminary declares, the "application of the Gospel to the political, social, and economic needs" of humanity is "secondary and subservient to [the Church's] primary spiritual commission."[8] Some Christians have become so engaged with the Lord they fail to become engaged with the world.

On the other hand, some folk are so focused on the transformation of society they neglect the transformation of their own souls through the regenerative work of Christ. Given the single-minded concentration of twentieth-century American evangelicalism on the inner life, it is not surprising that many socially involved church people drew away from overt expressions of affective piety. Dramatic conversions to a transcendent deity were replaced by religious nurture and education for social justice. Unfortunately, by underplaying the fervency of personal faith, social Christians have found it difficult to generate religious interest and enthusiasm among their ideological offspring. Eventually, the second or third generation of social gospellers have often felt estranged from a demonstrable piety.

Many social activists have had foundational, formative spiritual experiences at an evangelical church camp, youth group, campus fellowship, charismatic meeting, or Bible study, but have then "moved beyond" that kind of spirituality. One wonders, however, if the next generation will be able to find an equally life-changing faith when their mentors have neglected to provide them with any opportunities for expressing a personal commitment to Christ.

The socially conscious women and men depicted in this collection affirmed the importance and influence of affective Christian experience, despite the potential for its misappropriation. They understood the essential nature of the contemplative life in the work of social justice. They believed that initial, often dramatic, spiritual experiences were necessary to turn people from the love of one's ego to the love of God and humanity. "It took an emotional upheaval," Jones wrote regarding his conversion, "to carry me away from a self-preoccupied life to a Christ-preoccupied life."[9]

They also testified to the importance of daily devotion to God. The everyday work of social action demanded a profound sense of God's personal presence. A ready sense of spiritual access to God resulted in a bountiful resource for social reformers when they faced burnout from the perpetual struggle with structural evil. They knew that a continuous inward journey of faith must be at the heart of activism if it is to have any long-lasting integrity.

The second common element evident in the ministry of these persons was their vision of human interrelatedness. Through their varied life experiences, each of these Christians was shaken out of his or her ethnocentric parochialism and brought to a new place of support for the common good. For instance, the wholehearted affirmation given to Seymour by an integrated fellowship of Holiness believers in Cincinnati provided him with a practical model of interracial unity. Charles Stelzle's early experience of urban poverty instilled in him a lifelong commitment to the poor. Scudder's acknowledgement of the "plethora of privilege" encouraged her to identify with the dispossessed, and Jones's encounter with Indian culture helped him to realize his own enculturation and the need to de-Westernize Christian missions. In each case, these persons were drawn out of their cultural insularity. A new worldview was created in which they could visualize a community of mutuality.

One more shared feature was the way in which each of these individuals challenged the adequacy of religious institutions as they knew them. They were concerned that the church had compromised itself by its capitulation to the cultural entrapments of the surrounding society. For Goodell and Seymour, such a critique of established institutions was a fundamental part of their doctrine of the church. Both Goodell and Seymour longed for an egalitarian ecclesial structure in which traditional denominational divisions would be abandoned.

For the others we have studied, a critical assessment of religious organizations occurred unwittingly and was often contrary to their own predilections in favor of their denominations. Charles Stelzle loved the Presbyterian Church in which he was converted, but eventually his concern for industrial democracy drove him away from the doctrinal exclusiveness of his native denomination and toward ecumenical social involvement. Similar concerns motivated Jones's and Scudder's ecumenical interests. Jordan became so frustrated with Southern Baptists that he established an alternative Christian community.

The critique of established religious institutions by those who walked in the Spirit was related to their broader concern that American Christianity had accommodated to the secular values of the culture—to what Julia Foote referred to as "the maxims and fashions of this world." While they insisted on being engaged in the problems of society, they did not wish to be drawn into the market-driven mores of that society. Jordan reminded his readers of a Christian's responsibility in relation to the culture: "In the world, yes. But not of the world. . . . With an earthly mission to accomplish, yes. But existing on the face of this earth primarily to accomplish the purpose of God on the earth."[10]

If we intend, like these forebears in the faith, to walk in the Spirit, then we need to recapture the essence of their Spirit-led faith commitment. First, we must encourage significant Christ-centered religious experience. We should be open to the powerful transforming moments of God's self-disclosure,[11] and cultivate a daily doggedness of the spiritual disciplines of prayer and Bible study within an accountable Christian community. Some people today have difficulty responding to such practices. They may be concerned with how they will be identified, due to the current political and cultural associations with which this type of evangelical spirituality is aligned. But contemporary corruption should not inhibit us from claiming and restoring an American Protestant tradition that is genuinely ours to claim. Evangelical piety need not be self-focused or socially conservative; it certainly was not for the men and women who walked in the Spirit.

Also like them, we must acquire a nonparochial worldview, a vision of mutual interrelatedness. Overcoming prejudice against another race, gender, or class will occur only when we begin to view other persons as fellow subjects of God's grace—like ourselves, joint heirs with Christ. Politically, this multicultural mutuality can come about in America, according to activist Jim Wallis, through a "new politics of community" that will "aim at bridging our racial divides."[12]

Finally, we need to develop a healthy criticism of the prevailing culture, to be prepared to be a "loyal opposition" in relation to American government, economy, social structure, and church organization. In order for such a critique to have integrity, it will mean that—like Vida Scudder—we will abandon the seductions of "worldly" might and success for the sake of the reign of God. We may also be called on to challenge the "principalities and powers" of U.S. society—both secular and religious—and to have the courage and the will to try new structures and not to feel obligated to maintain the institutional status quo.[13]

Christianity and the Public Sphere

Encouraging American Christians to walk in the Spirit of a holistic religious commitment is made more difficult by the complex relationship that has existed historically in the United States between the manifestation of Christian faith and the articulation of public policy. Given the Constitutional separation of church and state, religious Americans have struggled to find the proper combination of devotional expression and social engagement in the civic arena.

The role of religion in the American public square had a particularly curious history in the twentieth century. Following the first World War, after the heyday of the social gospel movement, the only political cause to be advocated vigorously by Protestants was the prohibition of alcohol. But soon after Prohibition was enacted into law, it was deemed to be a miserable failure as public policy. The Prohibition amendment to the Constitution was repealed ignominiously in 1933. After this legislative embarrassment, most Christian leaders and churches during the middle decades of the century withdrew from direct political activism.

Meanwhile, mid-twentieth century politicians eschewed any public display of personal faith, except for an occasional vague reference to God for the purpose of advancing a generic kind of civil religion. Public figures denied that their specific religious beliefs made a direct impact on their political decisions. The quintessential statement of this strict division between religion and civic life was made by John F. Kennedy while he was running for President in 1960. In order to allay the qualms of those who feared the influence of his Catholicism on national policy, Kennedy assured a group of Southern Baptists that he believed "in a President whose views on religion are his own private affair."[14]

The change in the public role of religion from the 1960s to the 1990s is unmistakably evident when one compares Kennedy's frame of reference to that of Bill Clinton. When asked in 1996 about the role of faith in the civic arena, Clinton insisted that politicians ought "to try to live and act and follow policies that are consistent with their religious convictions."[15] Obviously, much religious water had flowed over the political dam in the thirty-six years between these two statements. In the interim, for instance, Jimmy Carter won the presidency in 1976 as a self-described "born again" candidate. During Carter's term, the American public became accustomed to a chief executive who mixed Oval Office politics with Southern evangelical piety. In a very different vein—but likewise combining religion and politics—Jerry Falwell and a group of fellow fundamentalists established the Moral Majority in 1979. Along with its successor, the Christian Coalition, the Moral Majority provided the conservative "Christian Right" with a political voice that they had not exercised since the 1920s.

Also in the 1970s, a cadre of socially conscious evangelicals, such as Orlando Costas, Samuel Escobar, Sharon Gallagher, John Perkins, Ronald Sider, Jim Wallis, Congressman Paul Henry, and Sen. Mark Hatfield, agitated for religiously motivated sociopolitical change on behalf of the dispossessed. By the 1990s, this set of visionaries had grown to include Christian activists like Tony Campolo, Roberta Hestenes, Eldin Villafañe, and Congressman Tony Hall. These progressive evangelicals began to find common ground with other similarly minded Americans who articulated a "politics of meaning."[16]

Unlike Pat Robertson and other leaders of the Christian Right, who wedded religious conservatism to cultural and political conservatism, the progressive evangelicals did not accept the dichotomization of the two-party system in American Christianity. Rather, these "dissenting evangelical voices" sought a unitive approach to faith and politics based on their reading of the comprehensive demands of the gospel. According to Wallis, their combination of "personal and family values with a commitment to social justice" led them "to embrace neither the liberal nor the conservative program." They developed "value-centered, community-based strategies" with a "biblical focus that transcend[ed] the left and the right."[17]

Advocating an integrated Christianity like that of the progressive evangelicals who walked in the Spirit will fly in the face of our culture's segmentation of life into sharply defined sacred and secular space. Such a spirituality will be fervently faithful and radically reformist. It will stress both evangelism and social justice, and it will understand God's relationship to humanity both transcendently and immanently.

Despite the fact that the existence of separate public and private spheres has dominated the history of nineteenth-and twentieth-century U.S. society, I contend that an integrated spirituality is culturally appropriate for American Christians. The religious ethos of the United States is not intrinsically and inexorably privatistic, as some have charged. To the contrary, the balance between the worth of the individual and the human obligation to others is inherent both in Christianity and in the democratic principles upon which the United States was founded. Though admittedly neither the U.S. government nor Christian institutions have consistently practiced their self-avowed principles, nevertheless there has been a continuous heritage of American women and men who have linked their devotion to God with their commitment to social activism.

Some may interpret the summons to practice an integrated spirituality as an attempt to find a moderate or centrist position between the opposing sides of America's "culture wars."[18] But integration does not mean moderation. In fact, if Christians merely advocate a moderating stance in relation to Protestantism's opposing parties, the result will be nothing but a bland mediocrity of the religious middle. Rather, a spirituality of integration will mean holding in tension the various aspects of Christian experience, a constructive dialectic between individual faith and social action. If taken seriously, both the personal gospel and the social gospel require radical repentance and conversion, a turning toward God and the world.

Devotion and Action

The chapel at Wesley Seminary, in Washington, D.C., is architecturally striking. On the left side of the chapel, a high massive wall of unbroken brick shields the congregation at prayer from the noisy city outside. In sharp contrast, a half-wall of clear glass visually dominates the right side of the sanctuary. The line of sight out the windows is directed toward Massachusetts Avenue, a busy thoroughfare that extends into the heart of the nation's capital. The chapel's left-handed monastic appearance reminds us of the need for devotion to Christ in the context of the worshipping community of faith, while its right-handed openness to the world destroys any illusions of withdrawing from human need.

Similarly, an integrative spirituality for American Christians will embrace the mutually reinforcing objectives of personal piety and social justice. Anything less will be inconsistent with the witness of the gospel and unresponsive to the pressing spiritual and temporal problems of U.S. society. By committing ourselves—through the power of the Spirit—to work for the transformation of both individuals and the broader culture, we will be instrumental in overcoming the two-party system in American Protestantism. More importantly, we will also be on the way toward a more holistic and Biblically faithful Christianity.

NOTES

1. Galatians is often referred to as "Luther's book."
2. Clarence Jordan, *The Cotton Patch Version of Paul's Letters,* (New York: Association Press, 1968), 102.
3. E. Stanley Jones, *A Song of Ascents: A Spiritual Autobiography* (Nashville: Abingdon Press, 1968), 67.
4. Orlando E. Costas, "Conversion as a Complex Experience: A Hispanic Case Study," *Occasional Essays* 5(June 1978): 37.
5. Ibid., 36.
6. As paraphrased by Ethel Dunning in Arthur Boers, "The Prophet or the President," *The Other Side* 24 (February 1988): 36.
7. C. Austin Miles, "In the Garden" (1913).
8. Wesley Biblical Seminary [Jackson, Mississippi], *Academic Catalog, 1996–1998* (Jackson, Miss., 1996), 8.
9. Jones, *A Song of Ascents,* 28.
10. Julia A. J. Foote, *A Brand Plucked From the Fire: An Autobiographical Sketch* (Cleveland: Lauer & Yost, 1886), 117; Jordan, *The Cotton Patch Version of Paul's Epistles,* 7.
11. See James E. Loder, *The Transforming Moment: Understanding Convictional Experiences* (Harper & Row, 1981).
12. Jim Wallis, "Who Speaks for God?" *USA Today* (28 March 1995): 13A.

13. Robert W. Lyon, "Abandoning Power," *Transformation* 3, no. 4 (Oct.–Dec. 1986): 10–14.

14. *New York Times* (13 September 1960): 22.

15. *George* magazine (December 1996). Ironically, Clinton's interviewer for the article from which this quote was taken was John F. Kennedy, Jr.

16. Michael Lerner, *The Politics of Meaning: Restoring Hope and Possibility in the Age of Cynicism* (Reading, Mass.: Addison-Wesley Publishing Co., 1996).

17. Wallis, 13A.

18. James Davison Hunter, *Culture Wars: The Struggle to Define America* (New York: Basic Books, 1991).